McKenzian Blueprint
ISBN 978-1-7380836-5-7
First Printing, 2024
PQADVANCEMENT PRESS
Ontario, Canada
www.PQADVANCEMENT.ca

EPISODE 1: THE ZANJ

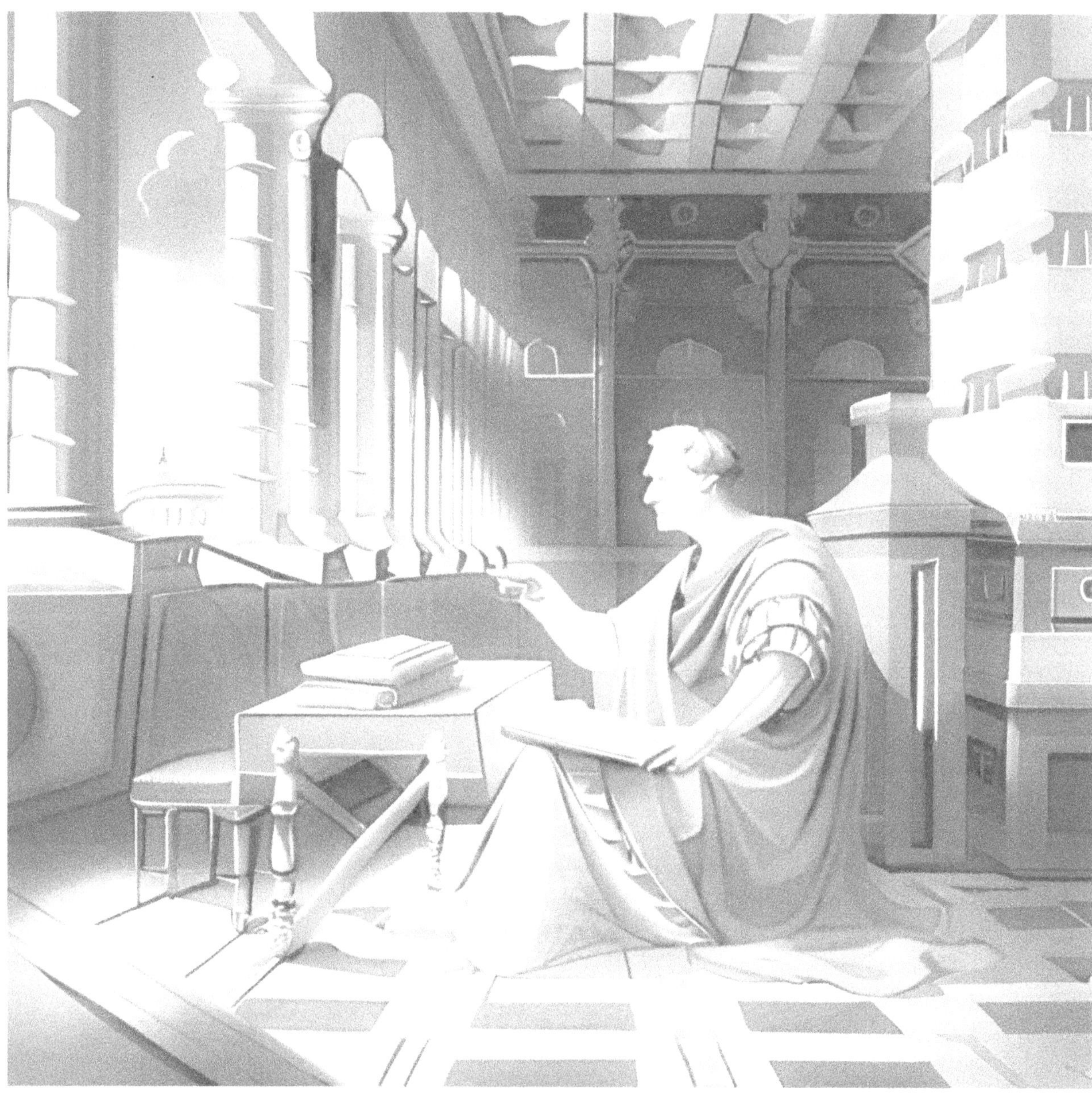

Azania is a region that is accepted by most scholars to be the name used by the Romans for the territory of East Africa which they visited and controlled in the first four centuries CE

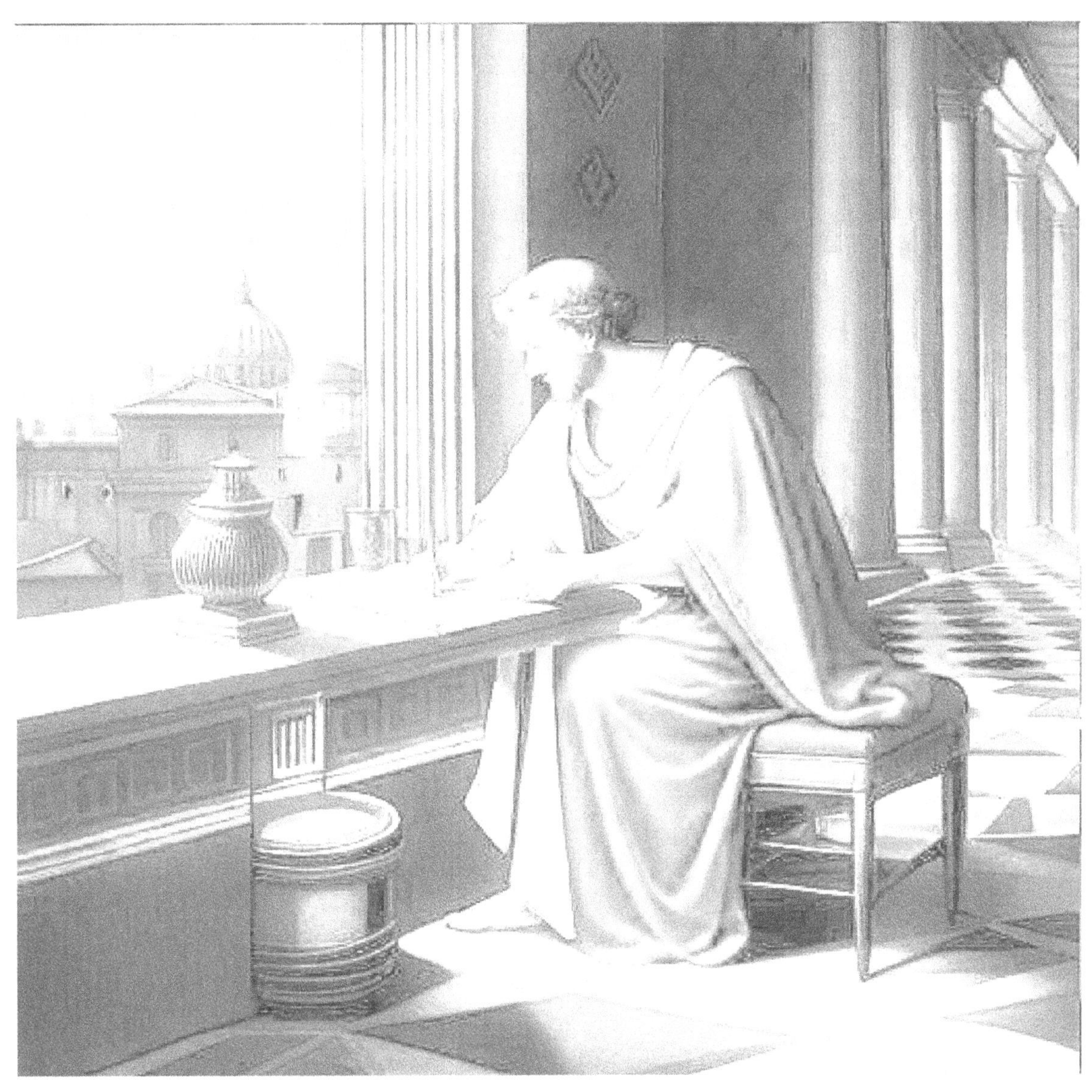

Azania was first mentioned by Gaius Plinius Secundus, famously known as Pliny the Elder, in the first century CE...

16th Century Trading Center in Mombasa...

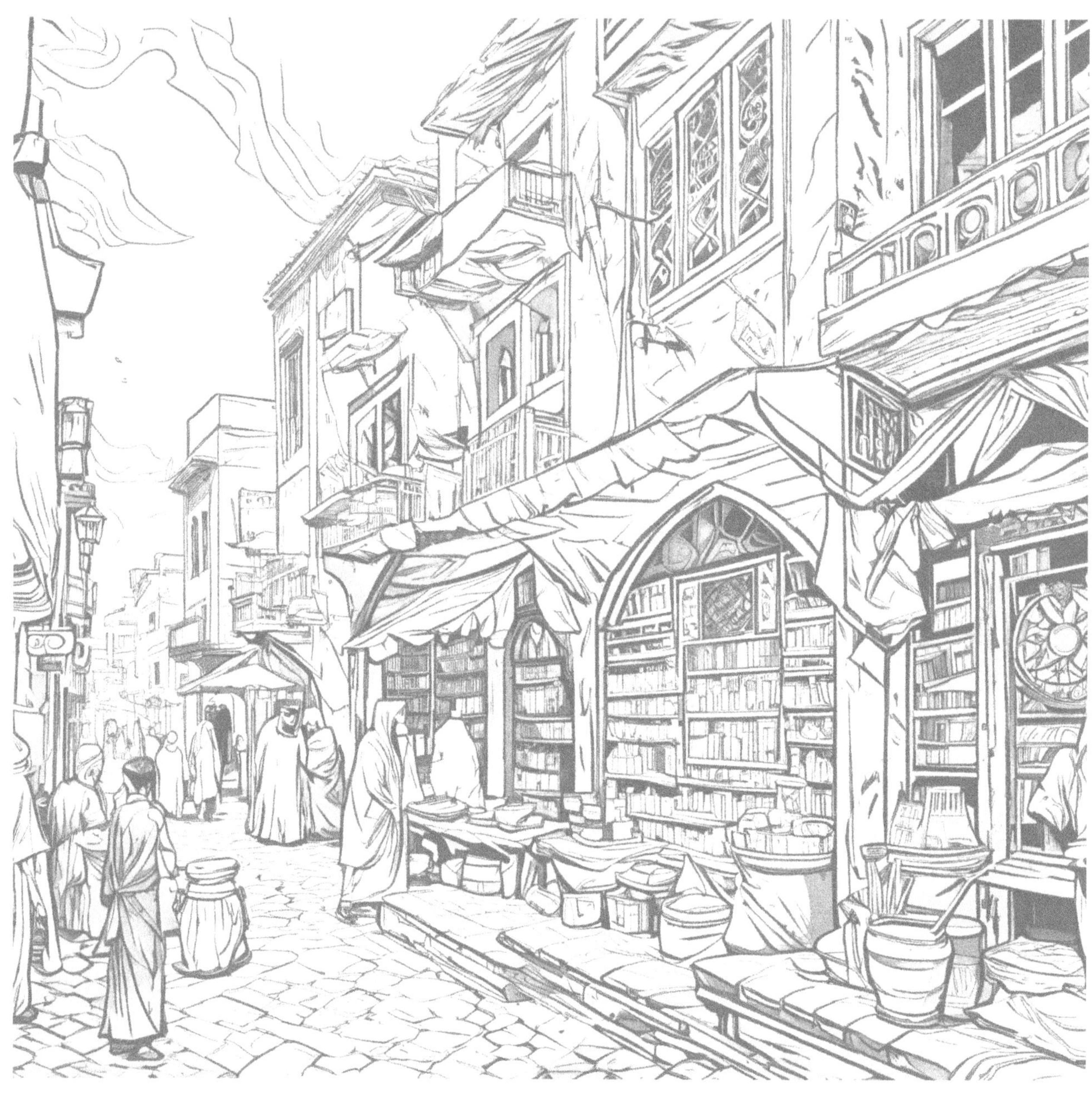

16th Century Trading Center in Mombasa...

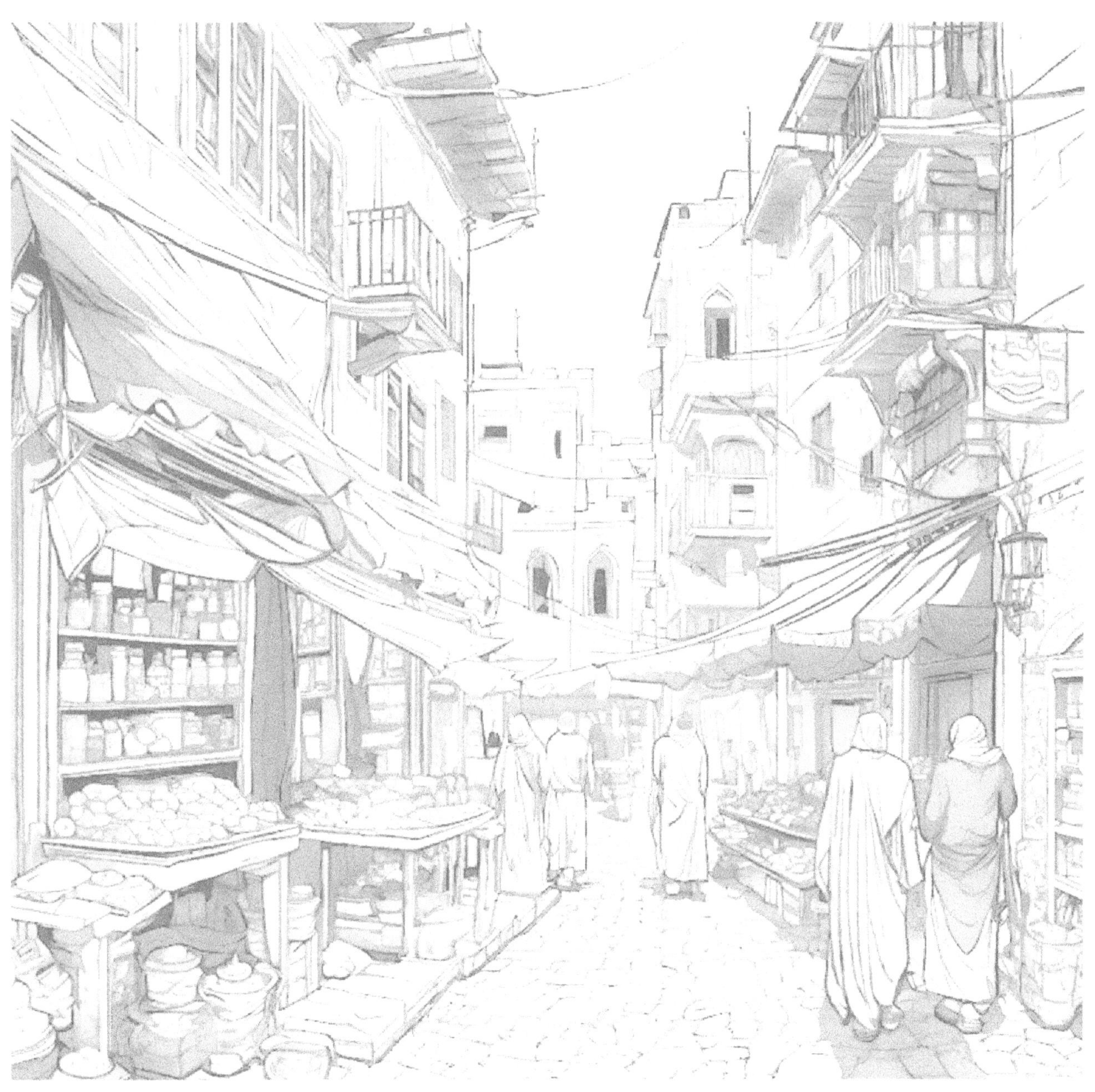

The Arabic identity for the East Africa region was 'Zanj' and is synonymous with the Zanj Rebellion.

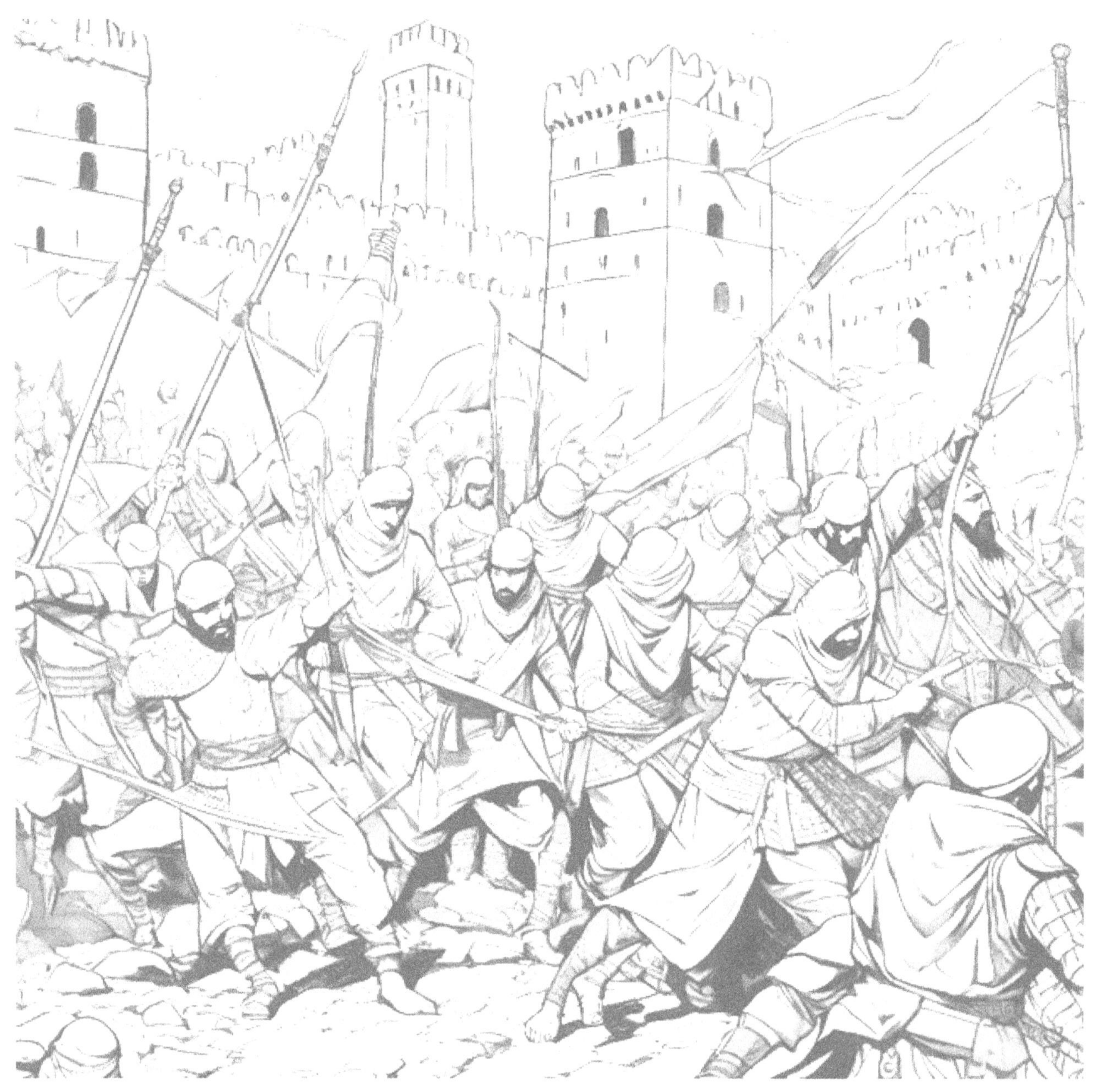

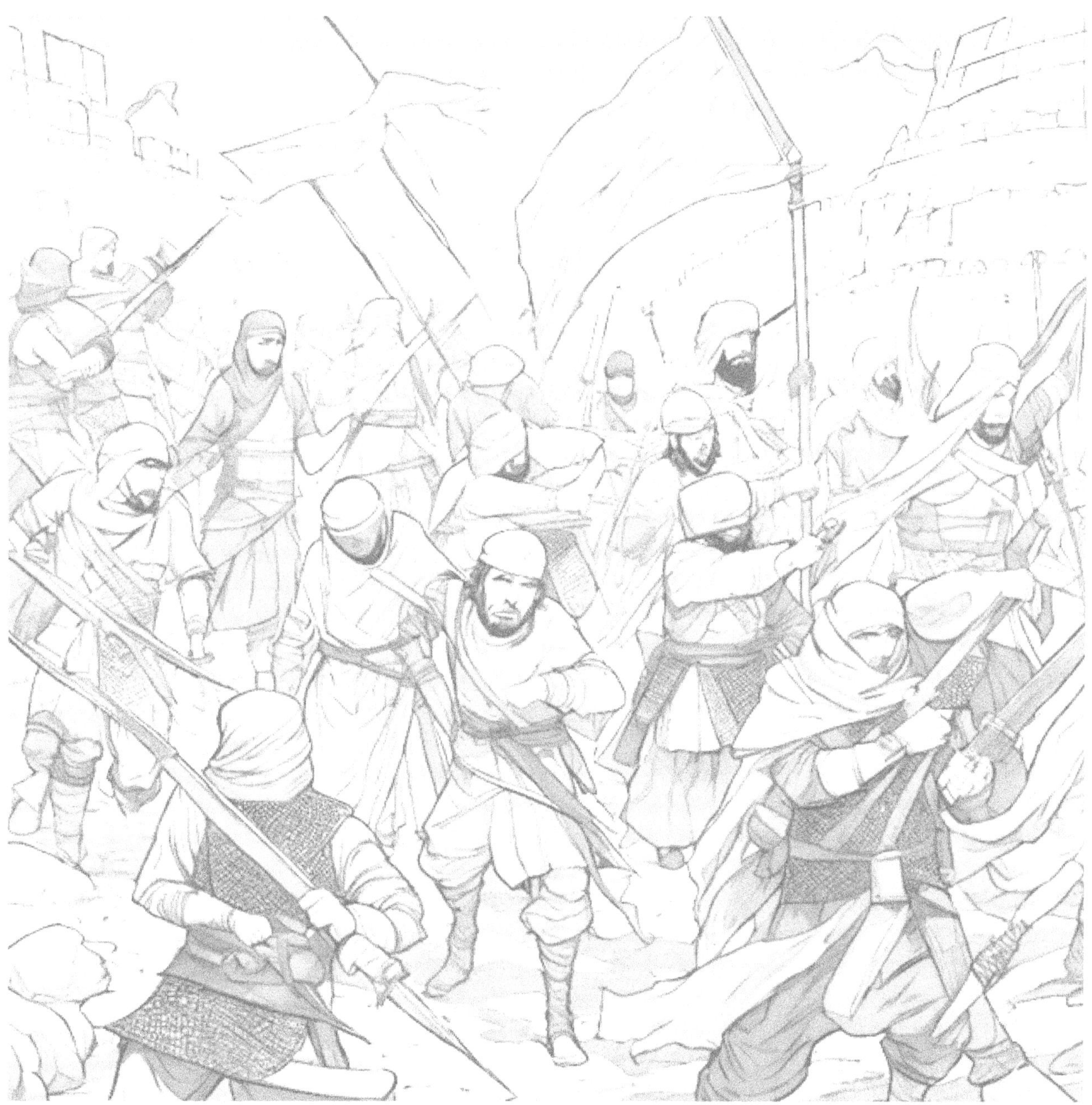

The Zanj Rebellion occurred from 869 to 883 CE in Basra (present-day Iraq) at the height of the Abbasid Caliphate

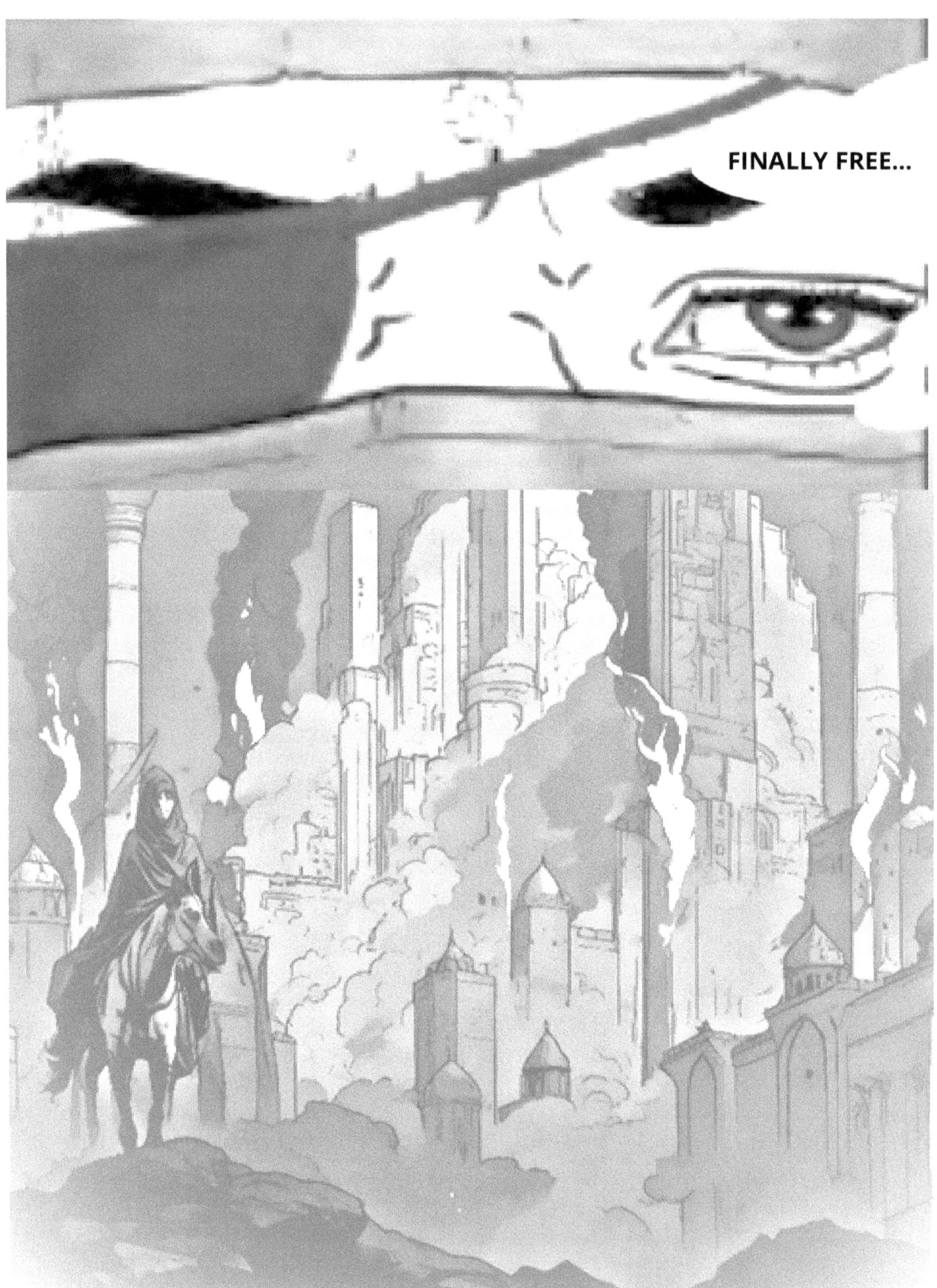
FINALLY FREE...

EPISODE 2: PORTUGUESE SUZERAINTY

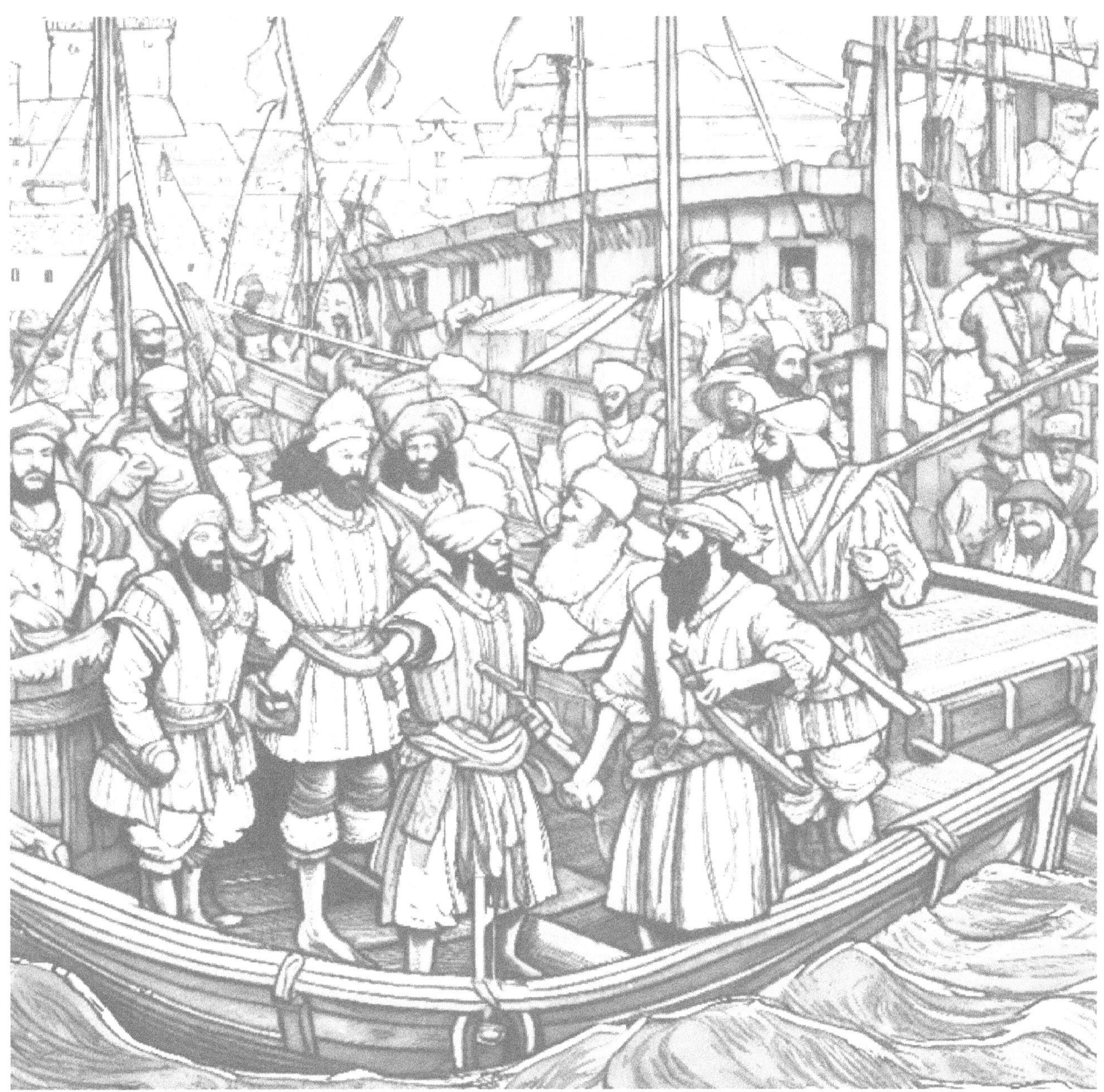

When Vasco Da Gama anchored off Mombasa in 1498, he found it to be a wealthy and prosperous town ruled by a Sultan.

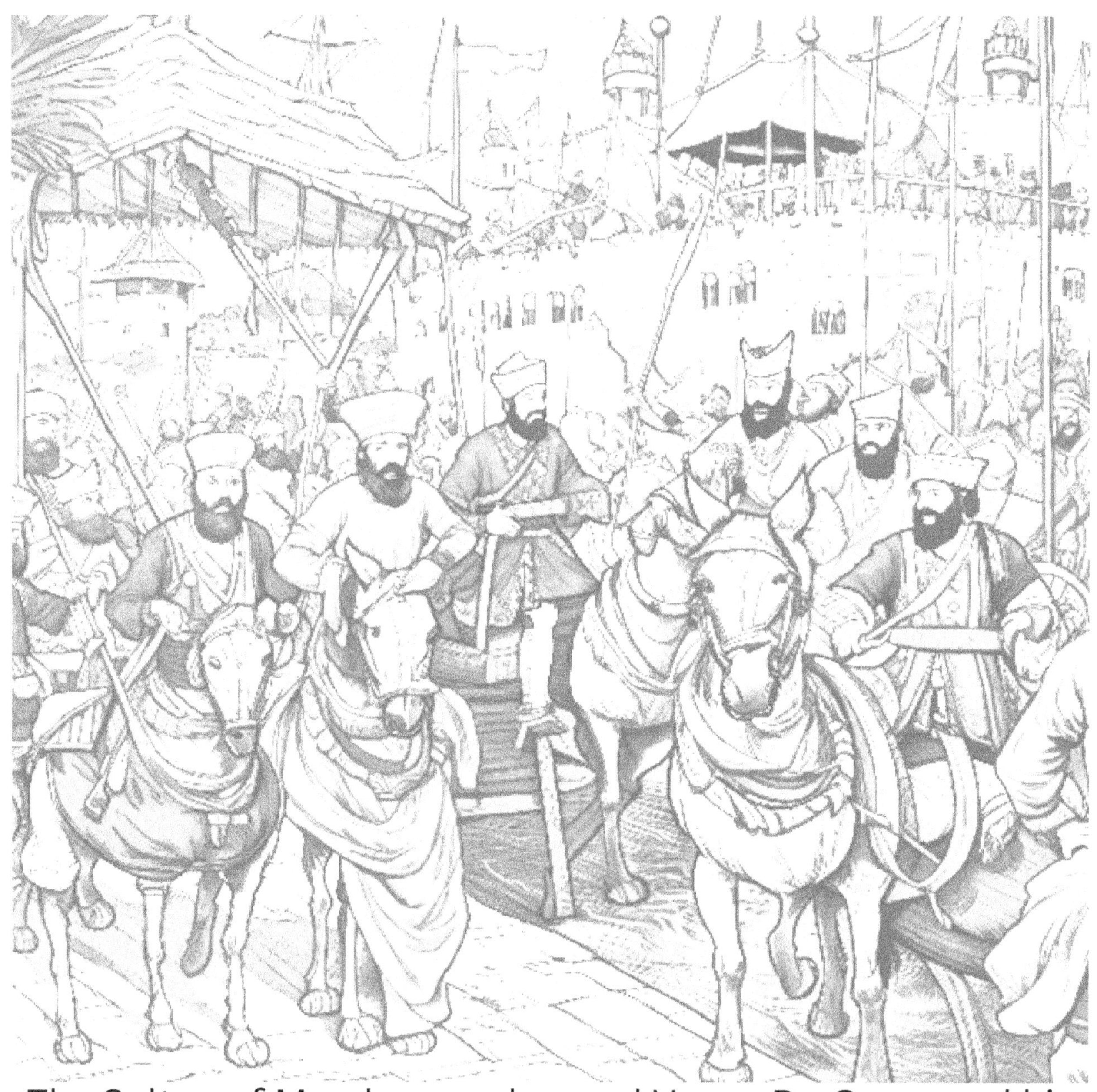

The Sultan of Mombasa welcomed Vasco Da Gama and his crew with honors

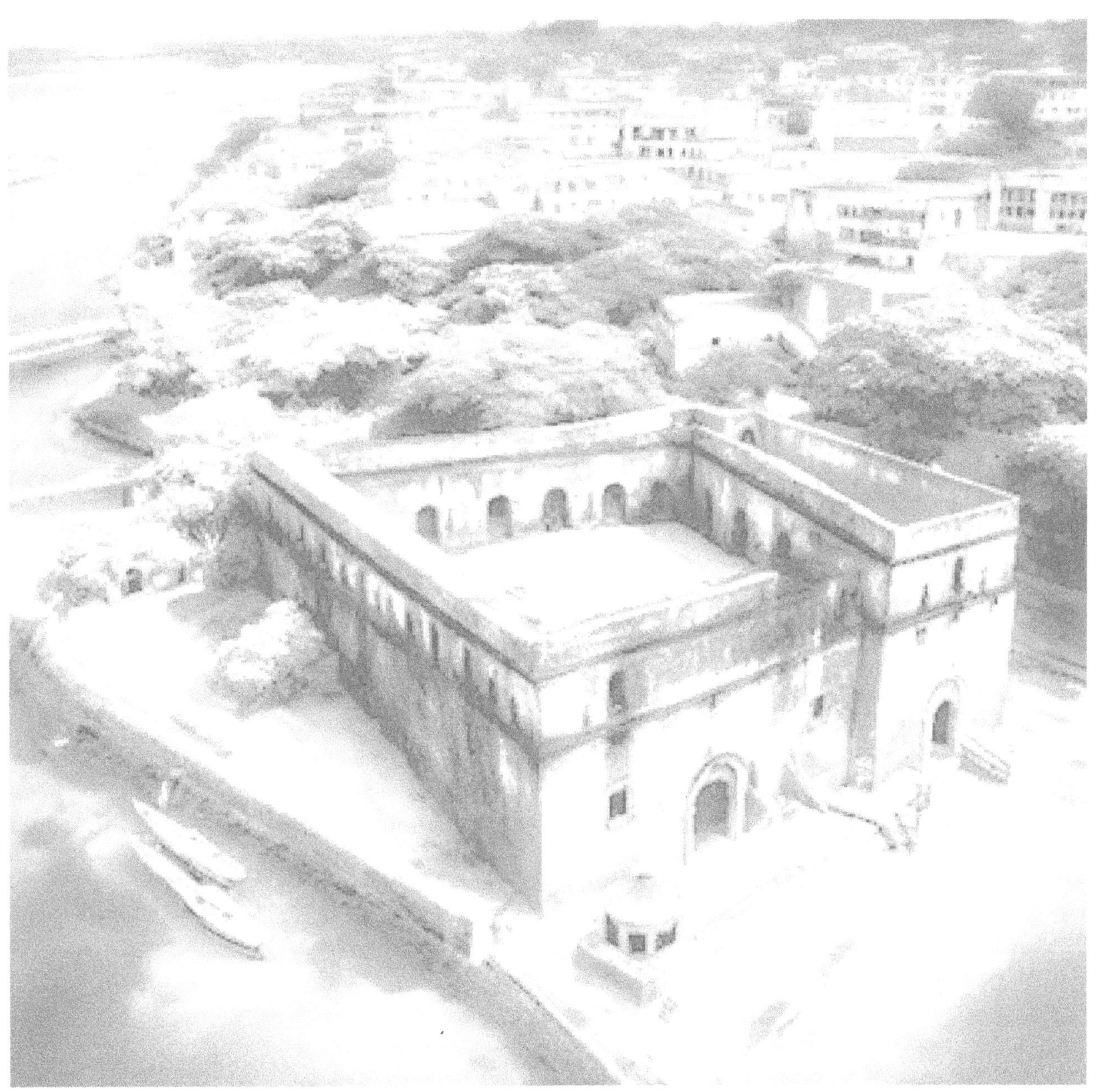

Fort Jesus in Mombasa

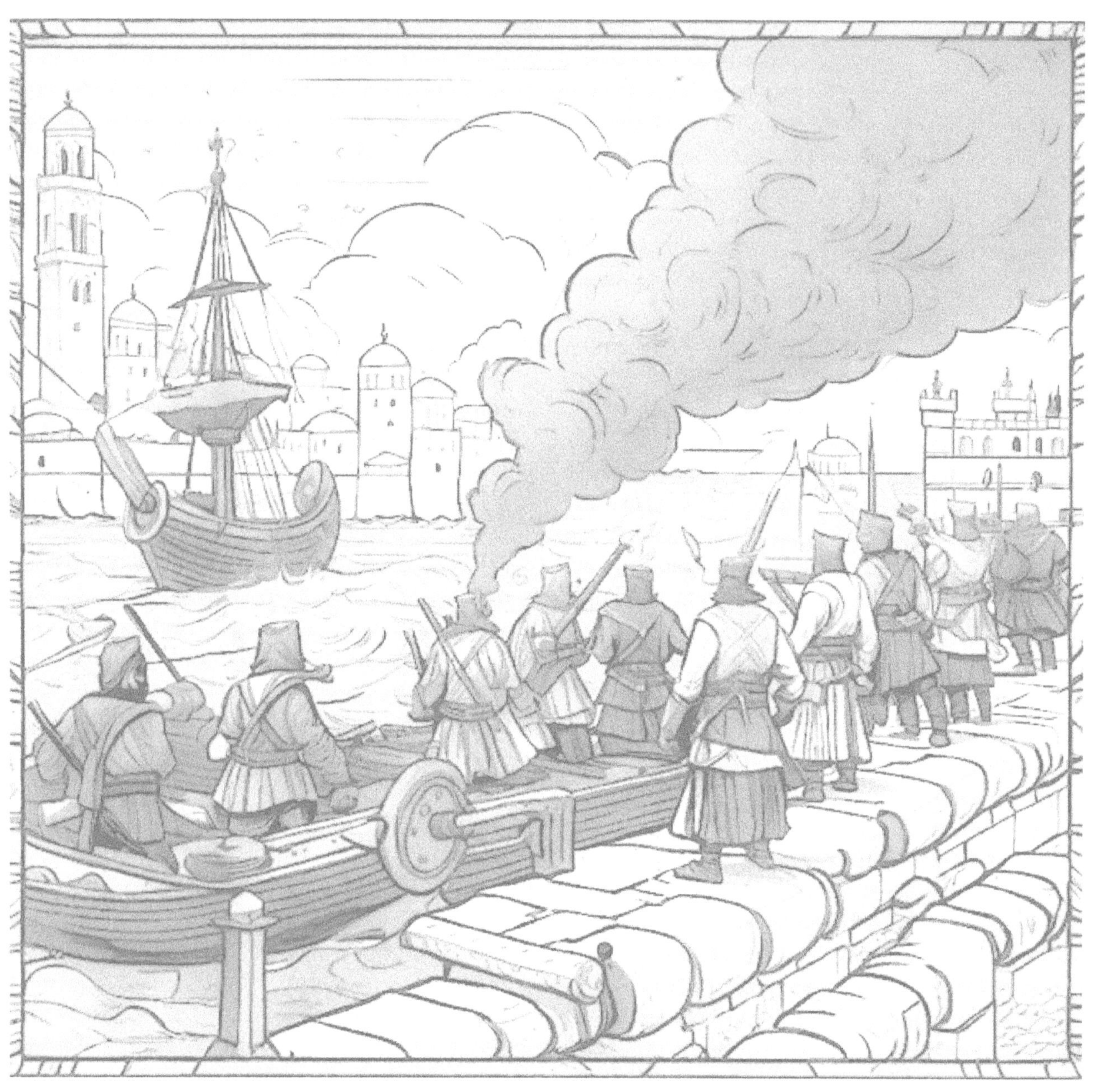

Naval might established rights. Vasco Da Gama orchestrated the attack of Mombasa by Pedro Álvares Cabral in 1500 and again in 1505 by Francisco de Almeida, the first Portuguese Viceroy of India.

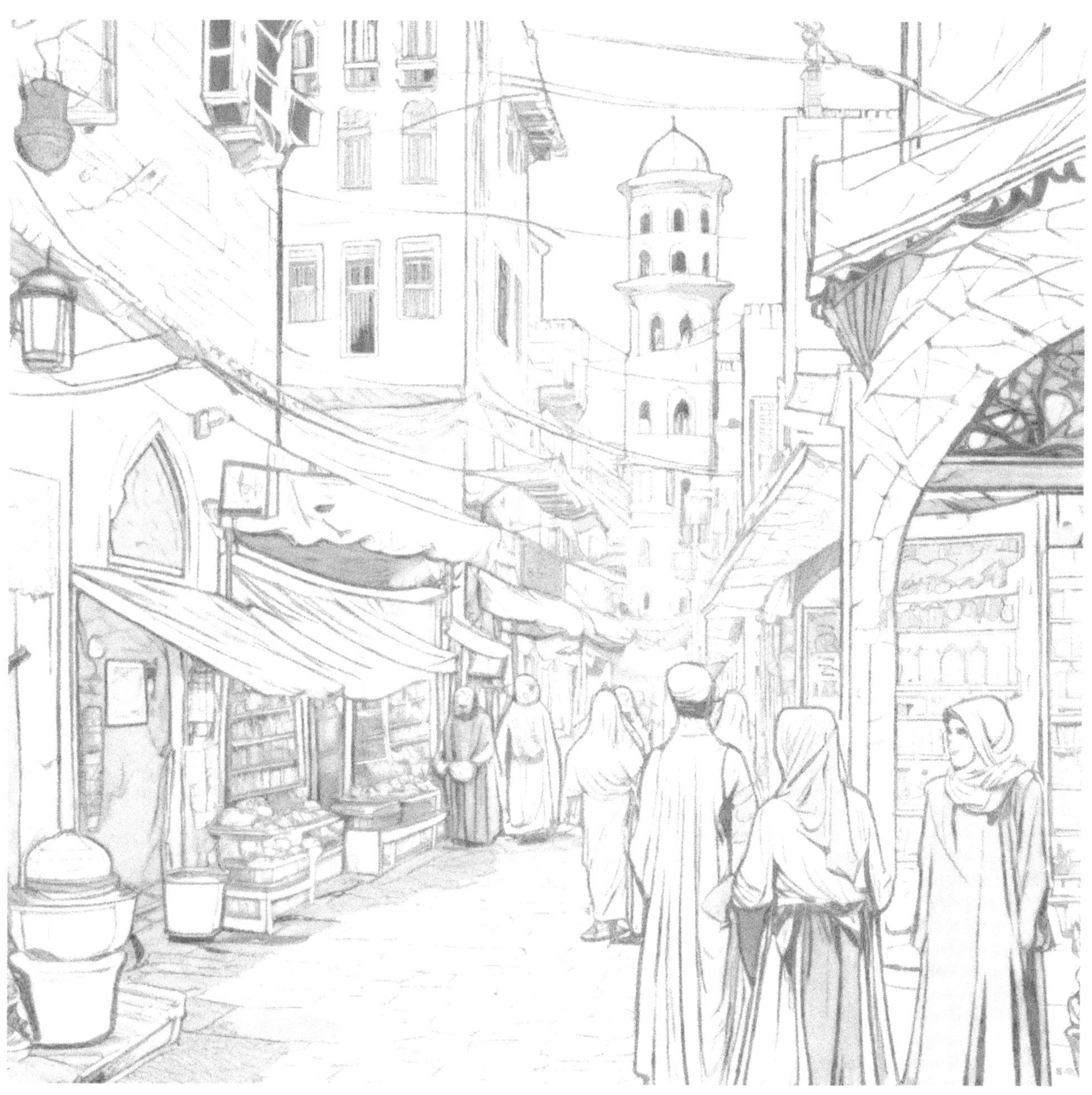

The Sultan of Mombasa became a tributary of Portugal and ruled by decree.

EPISODE 3: OMANI ARABS

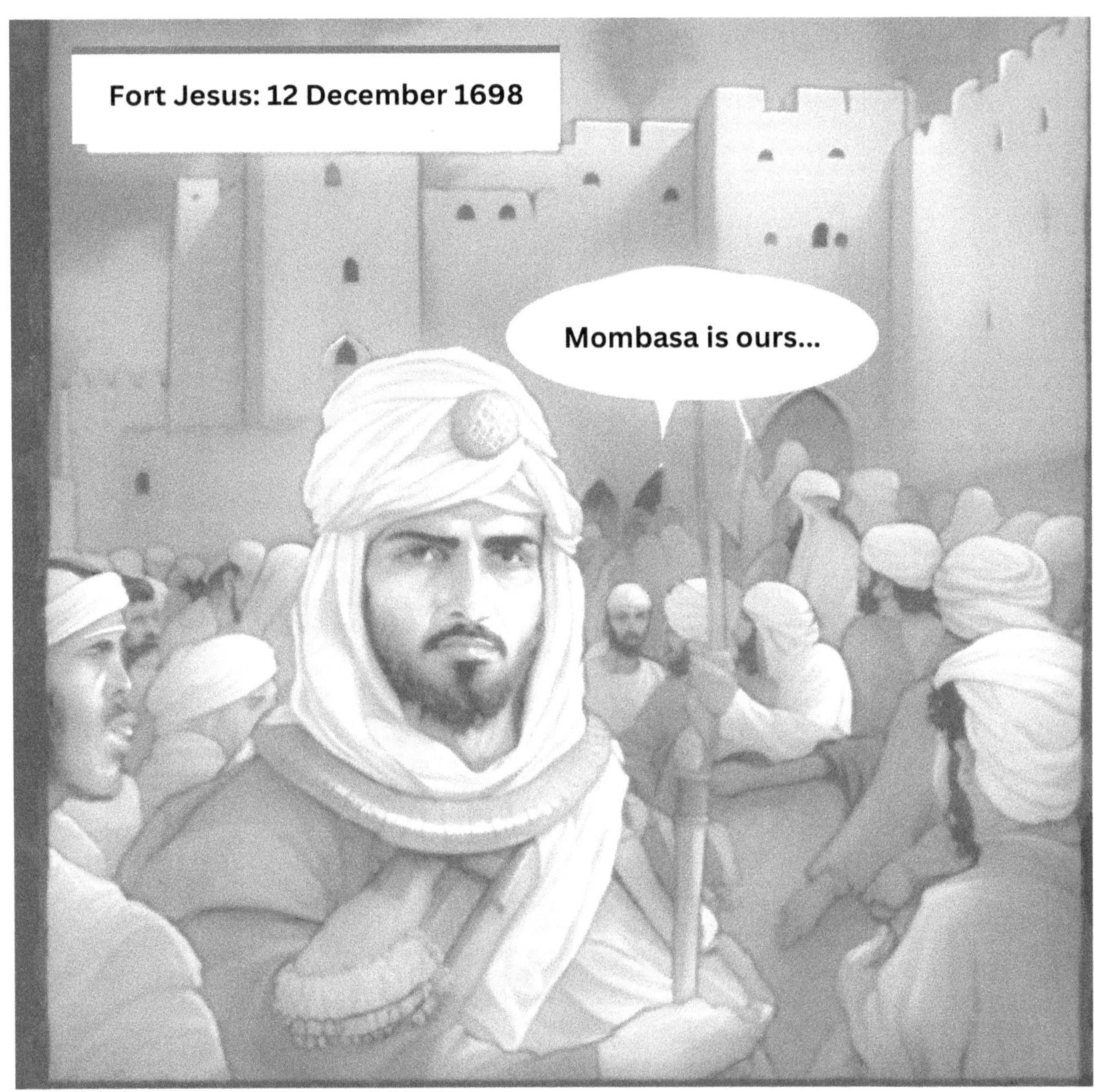

The Omani Arabs stormed and took Fort Jesus after a 33-month siege

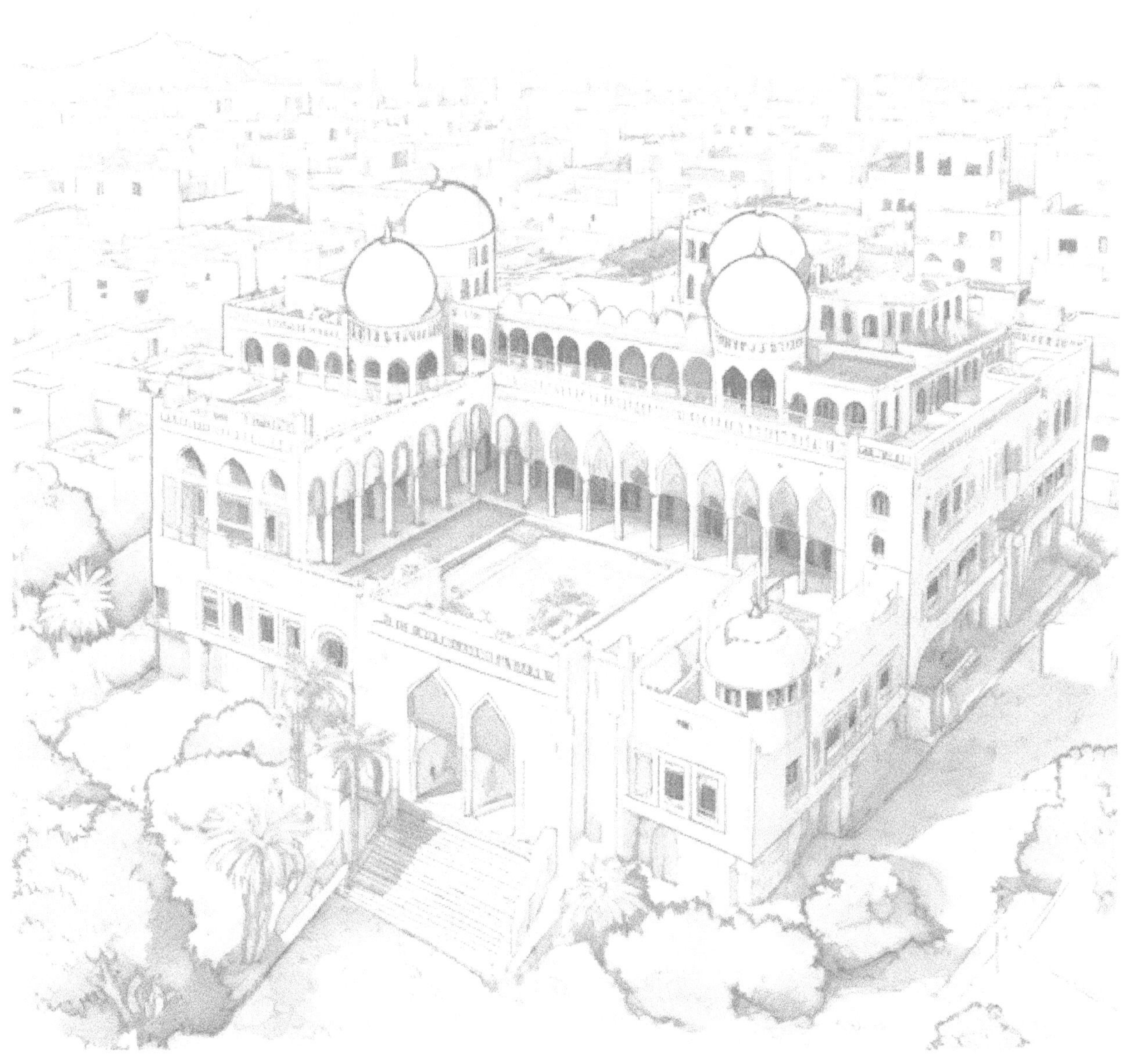

In 1749, the Yarubi were replaced as the ruling family in Muscat by the Al Busaidi, from whom the Sultans of Zanzibar are descended

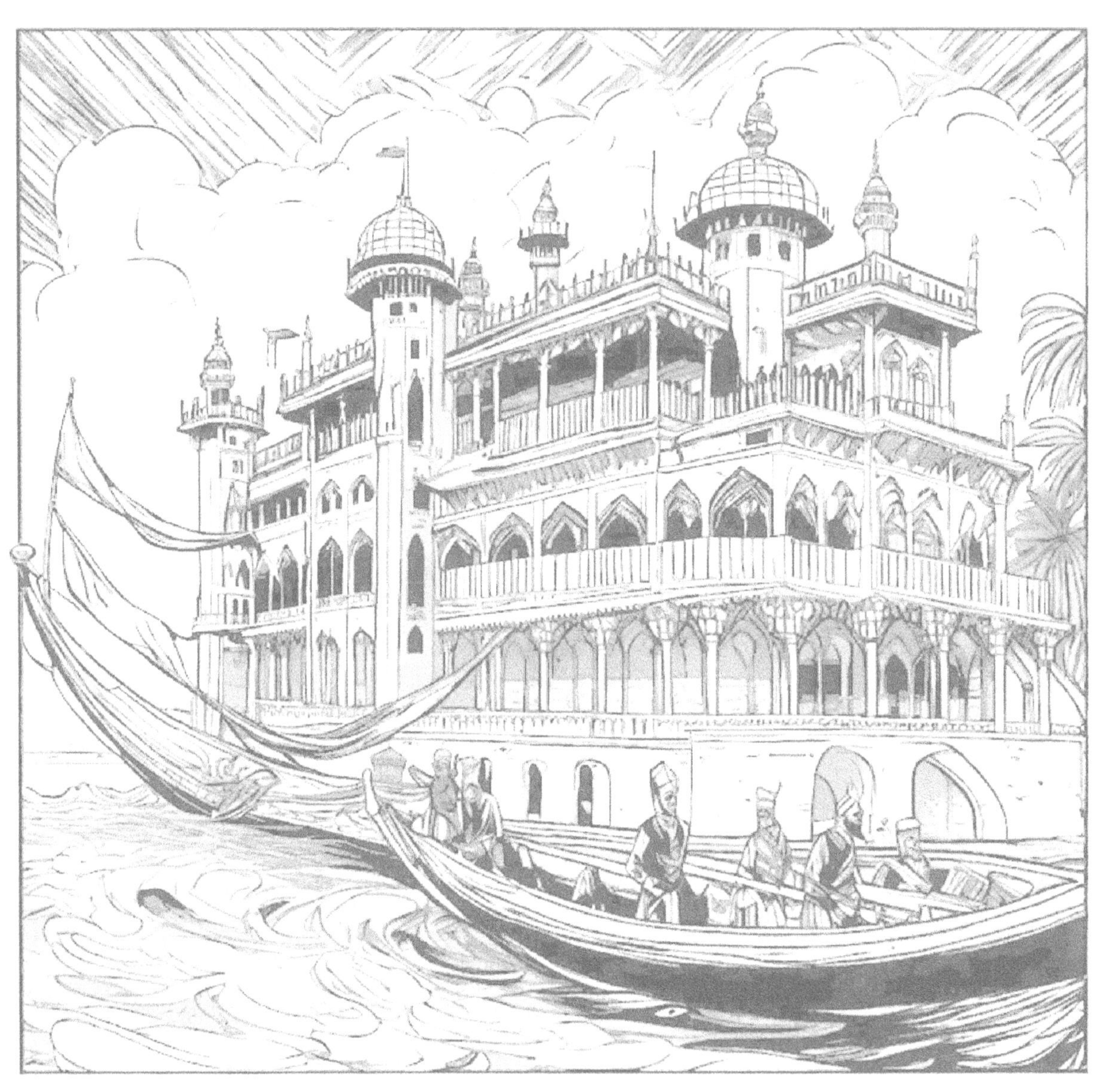

In 1785, the Imam Ahmad bin Said visited Mombasa and compelled the Mazruis, who were governing on his behalf, to recognize him as their sovereign

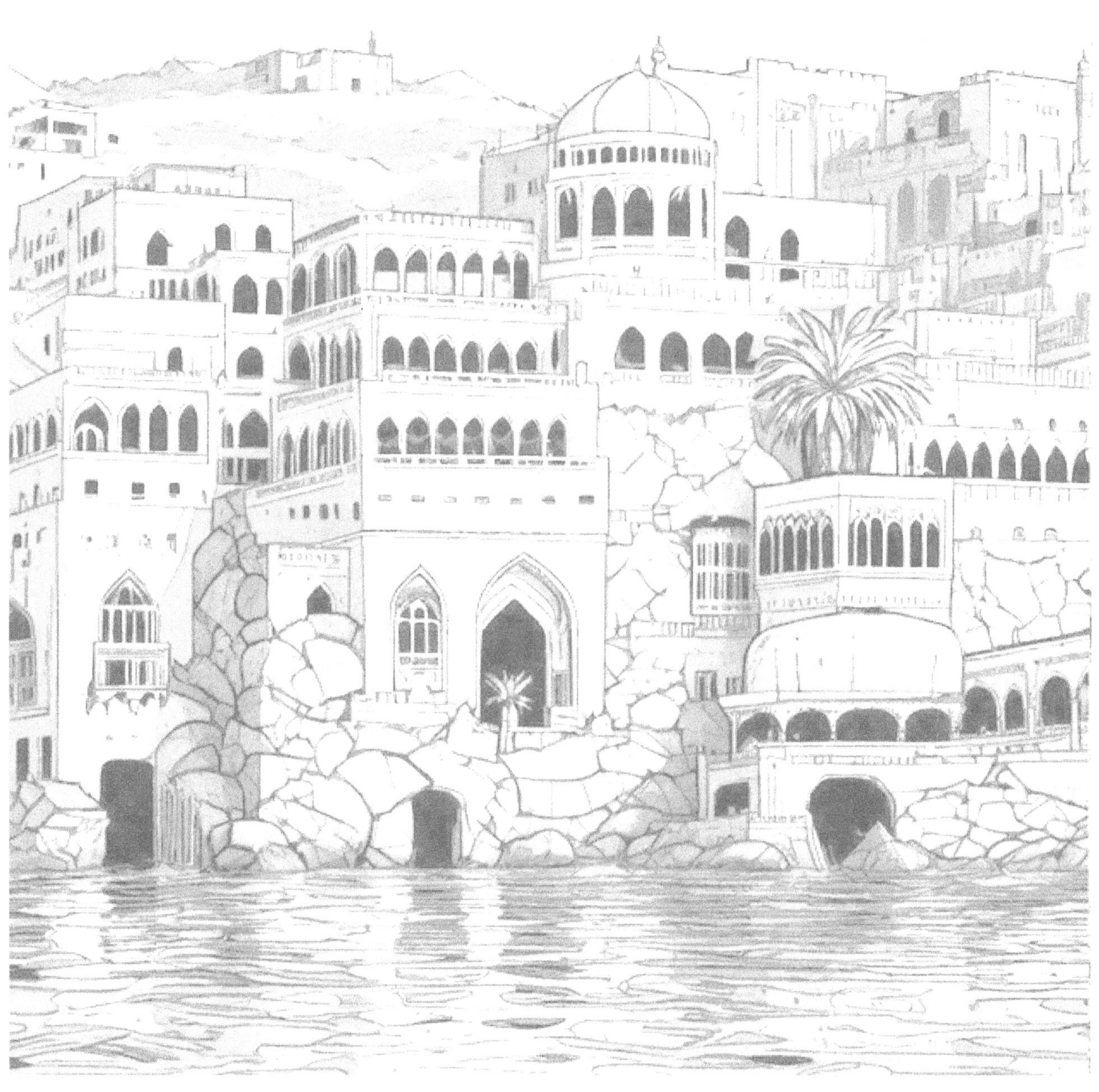

The Lamu Fort was built between 1813 - 1821 under the Omani Arabs

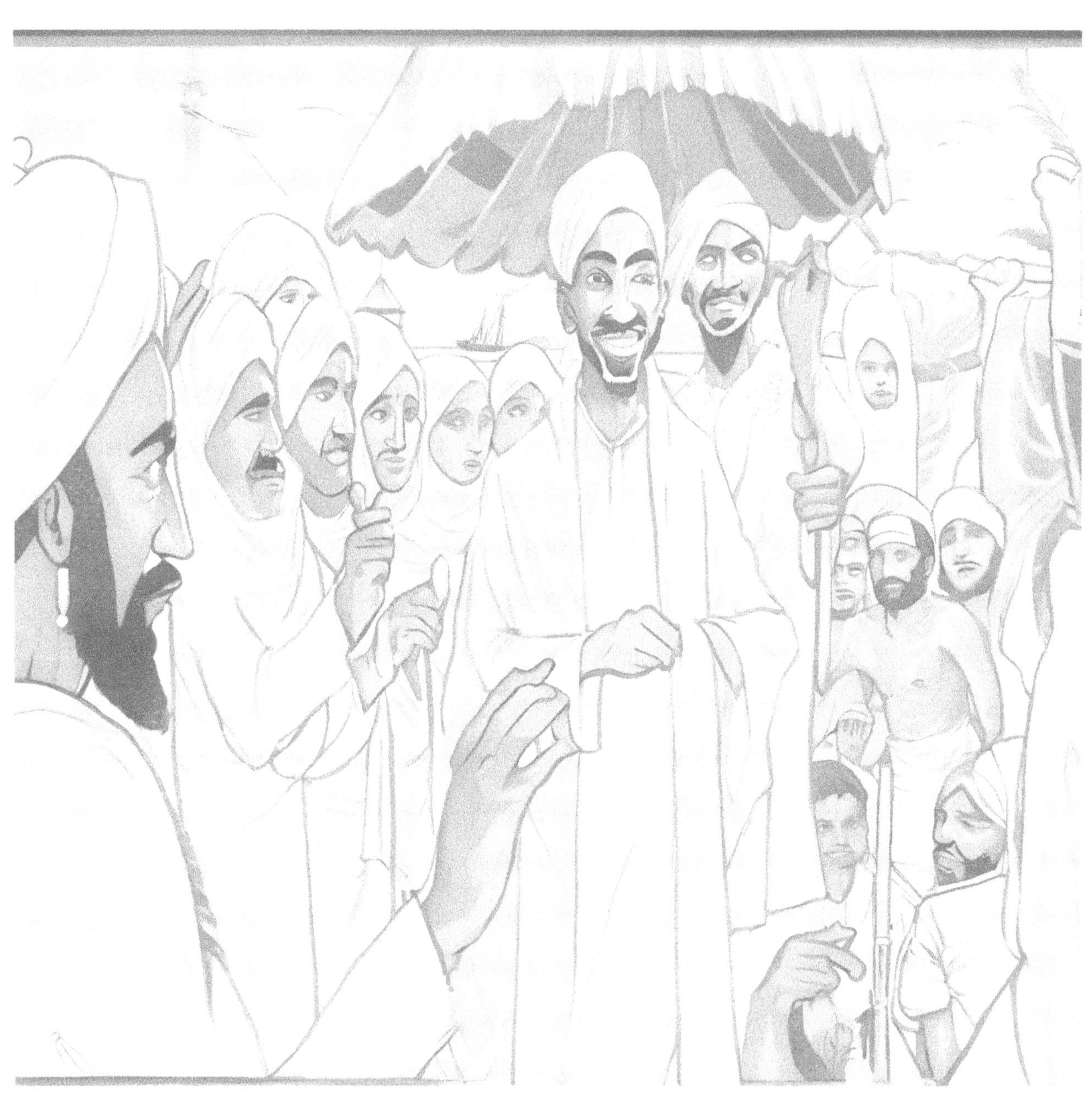

In 1832 Seyyid Said settled in Zanzibar and moved his capital from Oman (Muscat) to Zanzibar in 1840

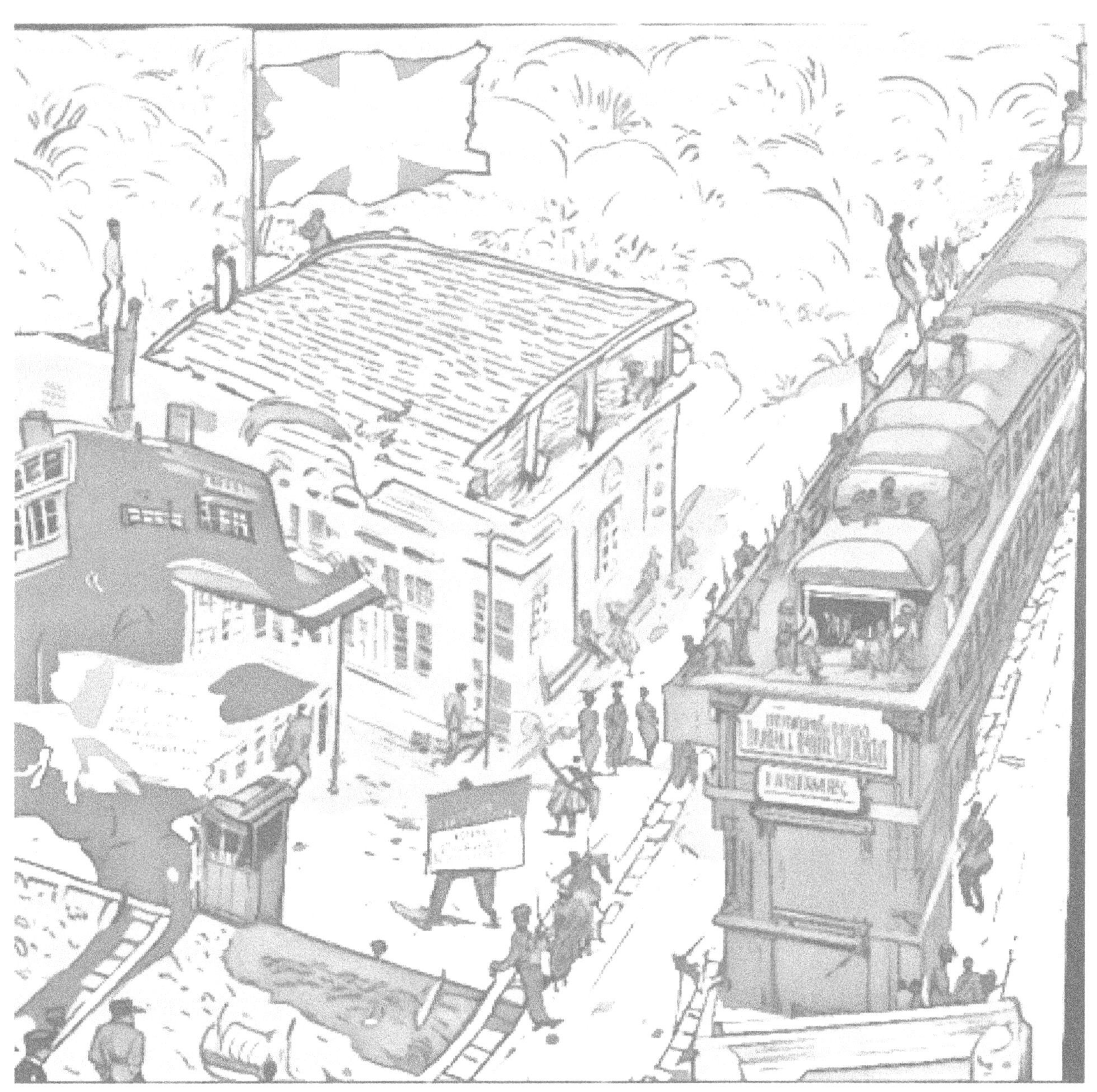

With incessant dissent from the Mazrui governors, the Sultan of Zanzibar made overtures to the British to help route them in 1895...

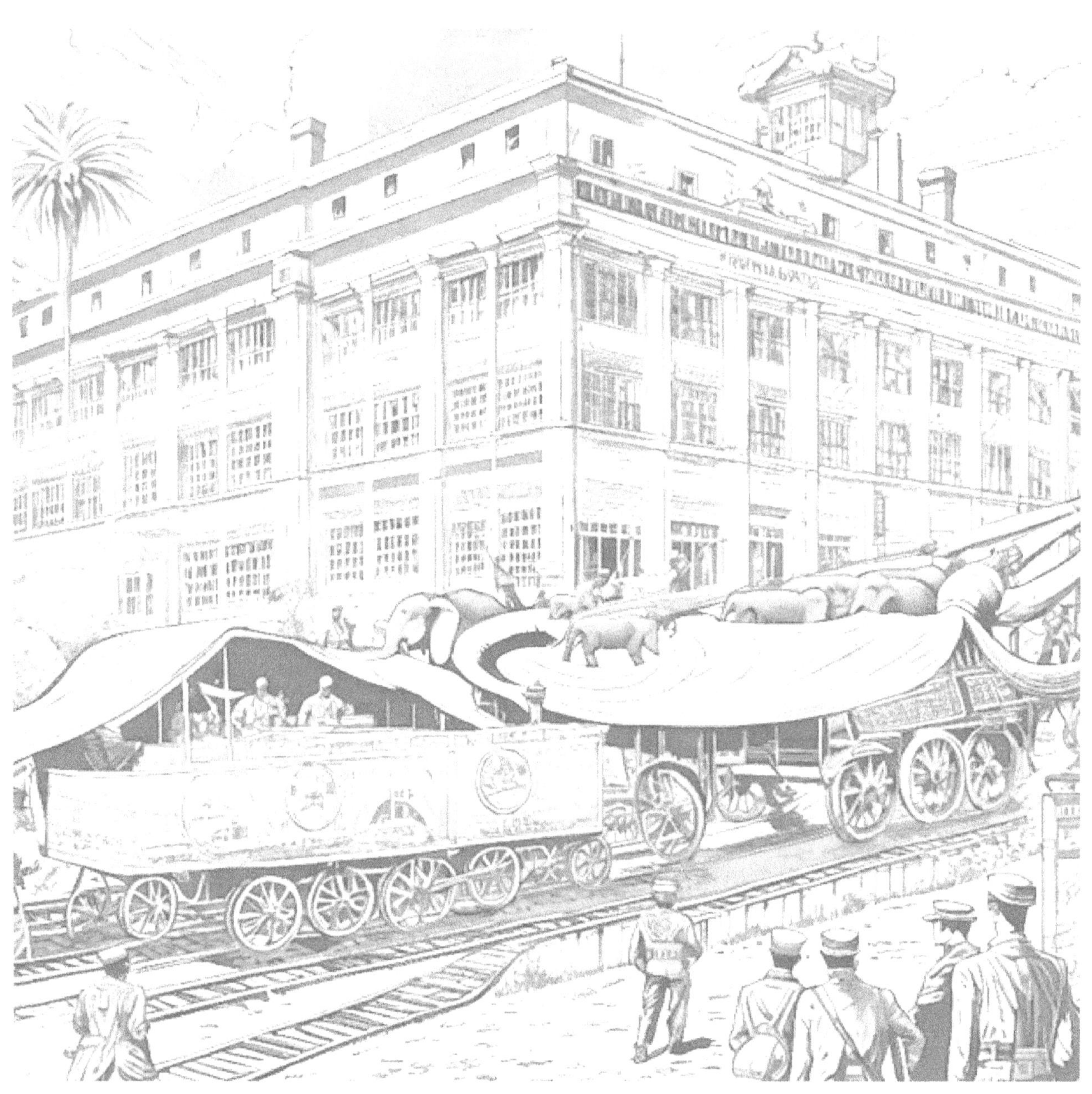

The 1895 Mazrui Rebellion saw the Imperial British East Africa Company gain concession to the port of entry in Mombasa.

EPISODE 4: EAST AFRICA PROTECTORATE

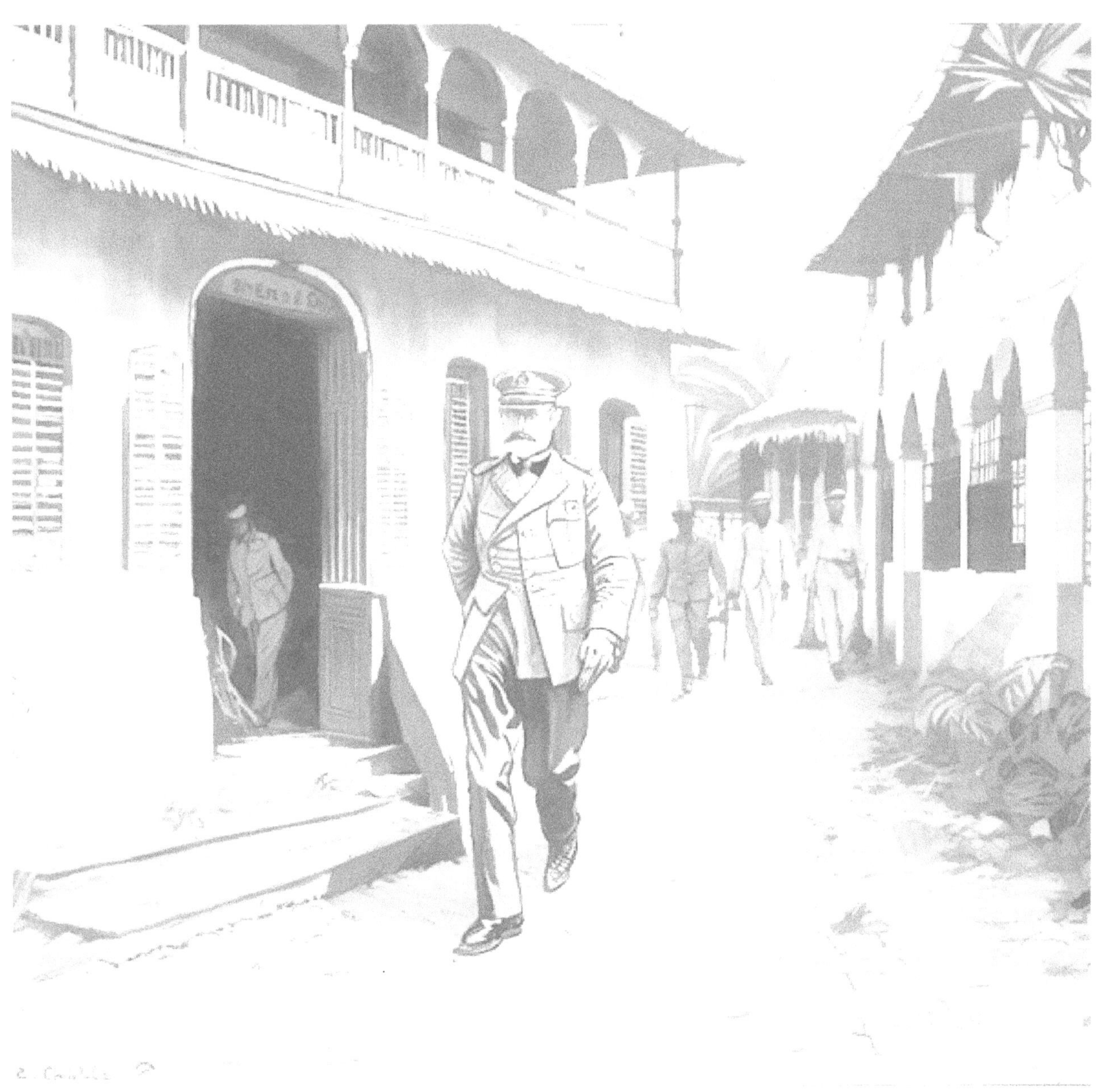

When Sir Charles Eliot became Commissioner of British East Africa in 1900-1904, he undertook extensive tours of the hinterland...

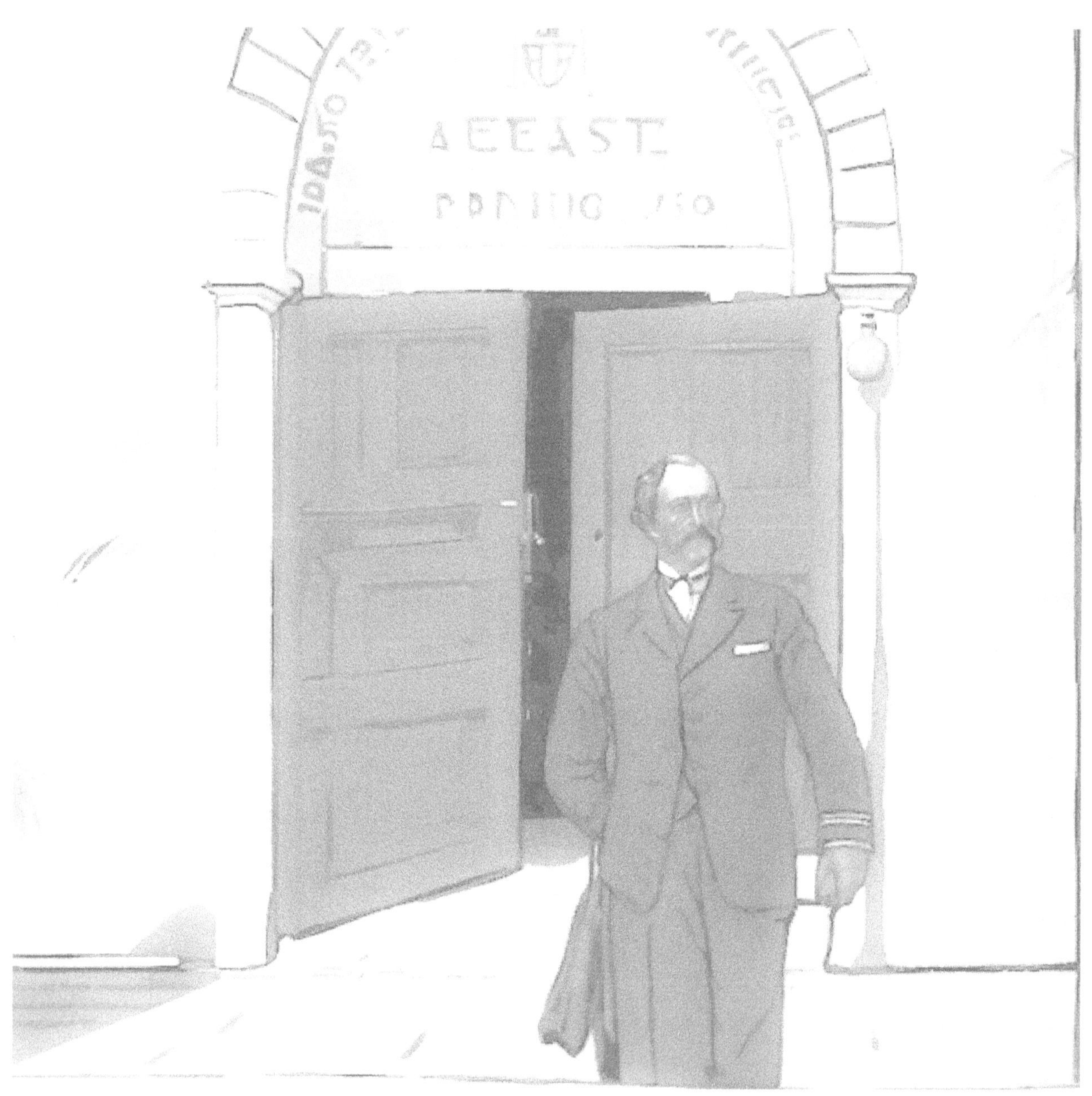

Sir Charles Eliot interacted with the locals upon which he developed an elaborate report identifying settlement areas for the British.

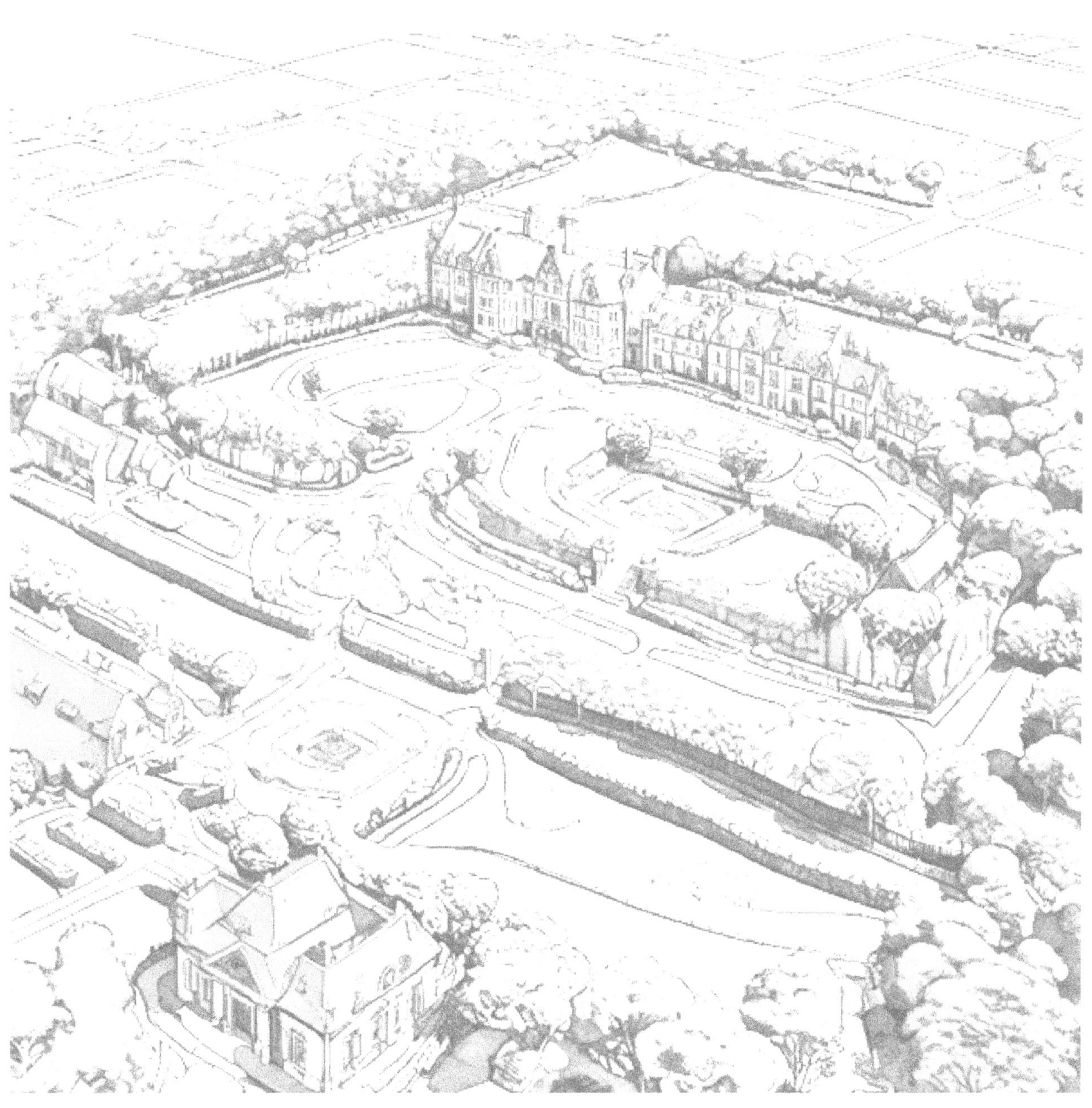

Hugh Cholmondeley inherited the Barony of Delamere and the Vale Royal estate in Cheshire in 1887 while aged seventeen.

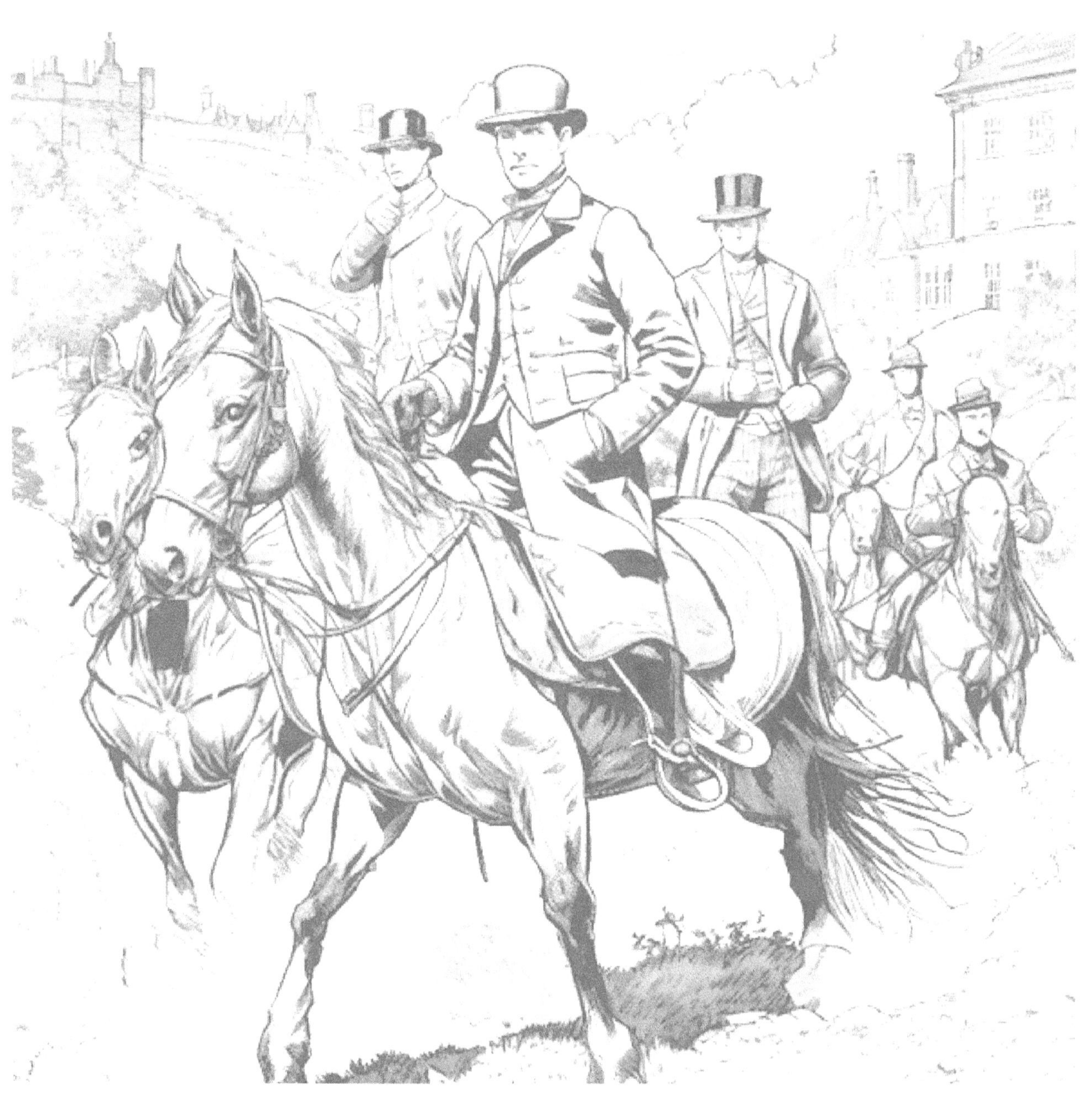

Hugh Cholmondeley at the Vale Royal estate in Cheshire in 1887.

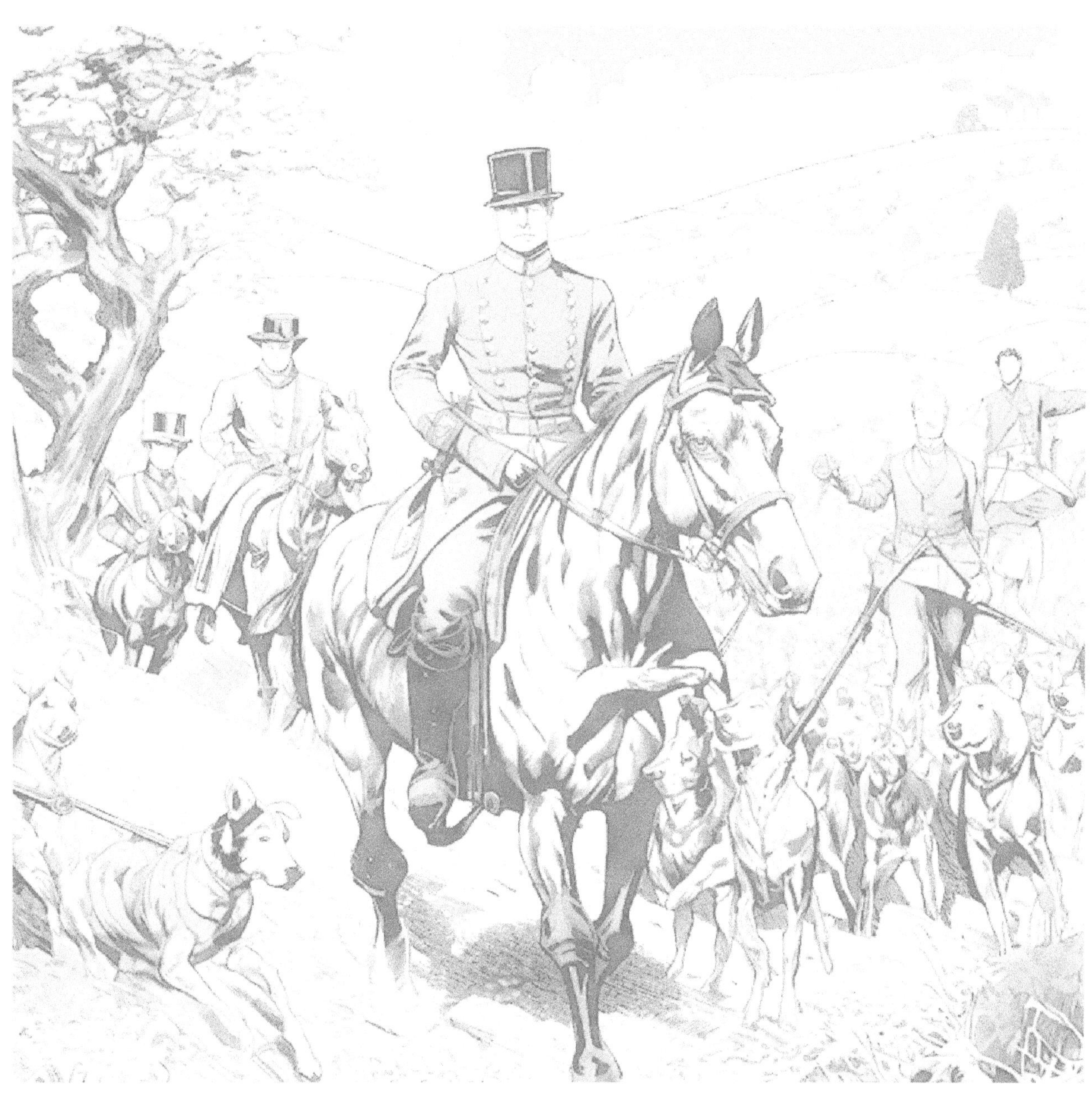

In 1897-8, the 3rd Baron Delamere, traveled with his friend Dr. Atkinson to the East Africa Protectorate on a hunting expedition, emerging at Lake Rudolf (now Lake Turkana).

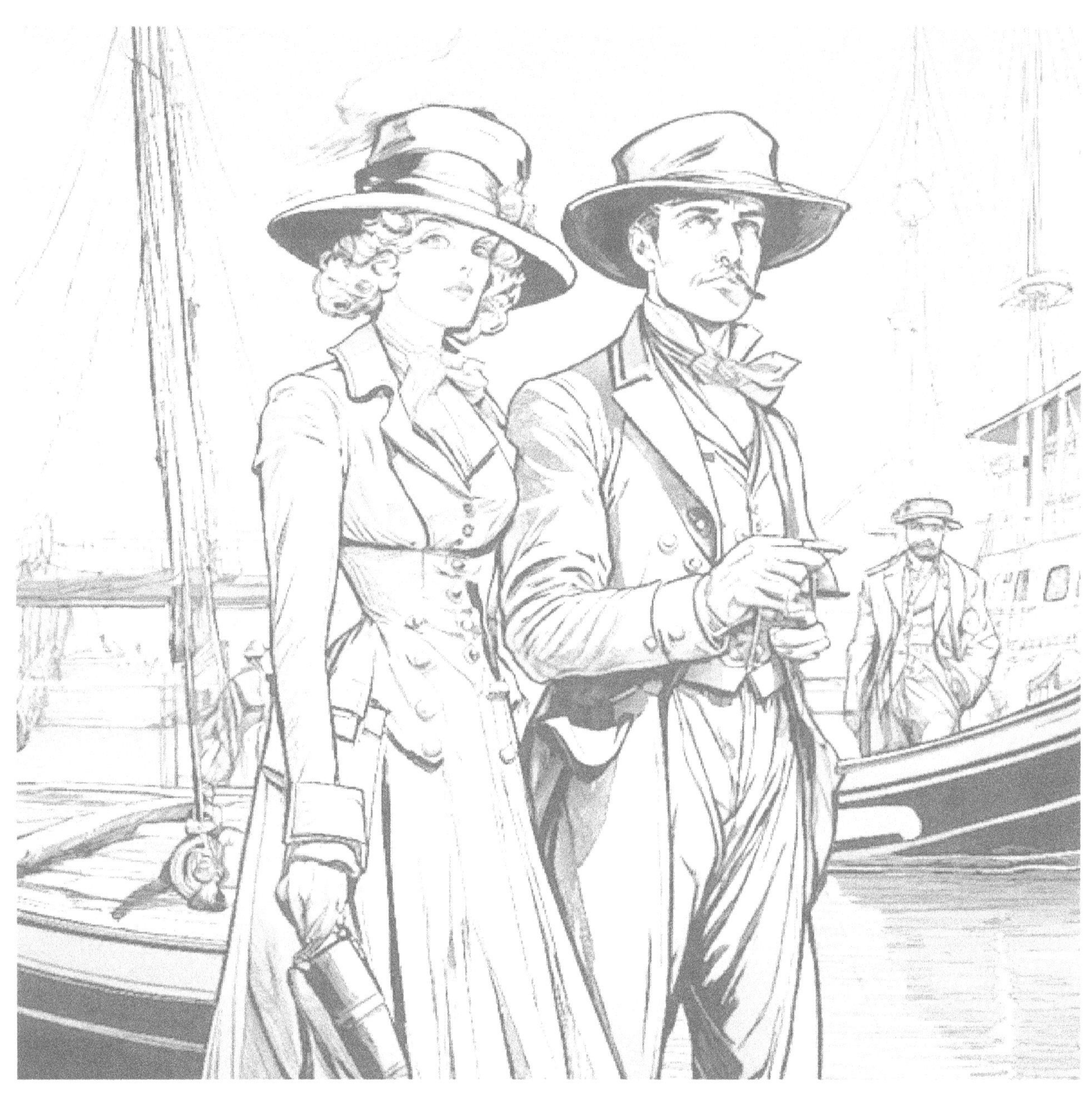

Lord Delamere returned to the East Africa Protectorate in 1902 with his wife, Lady Florence Cole

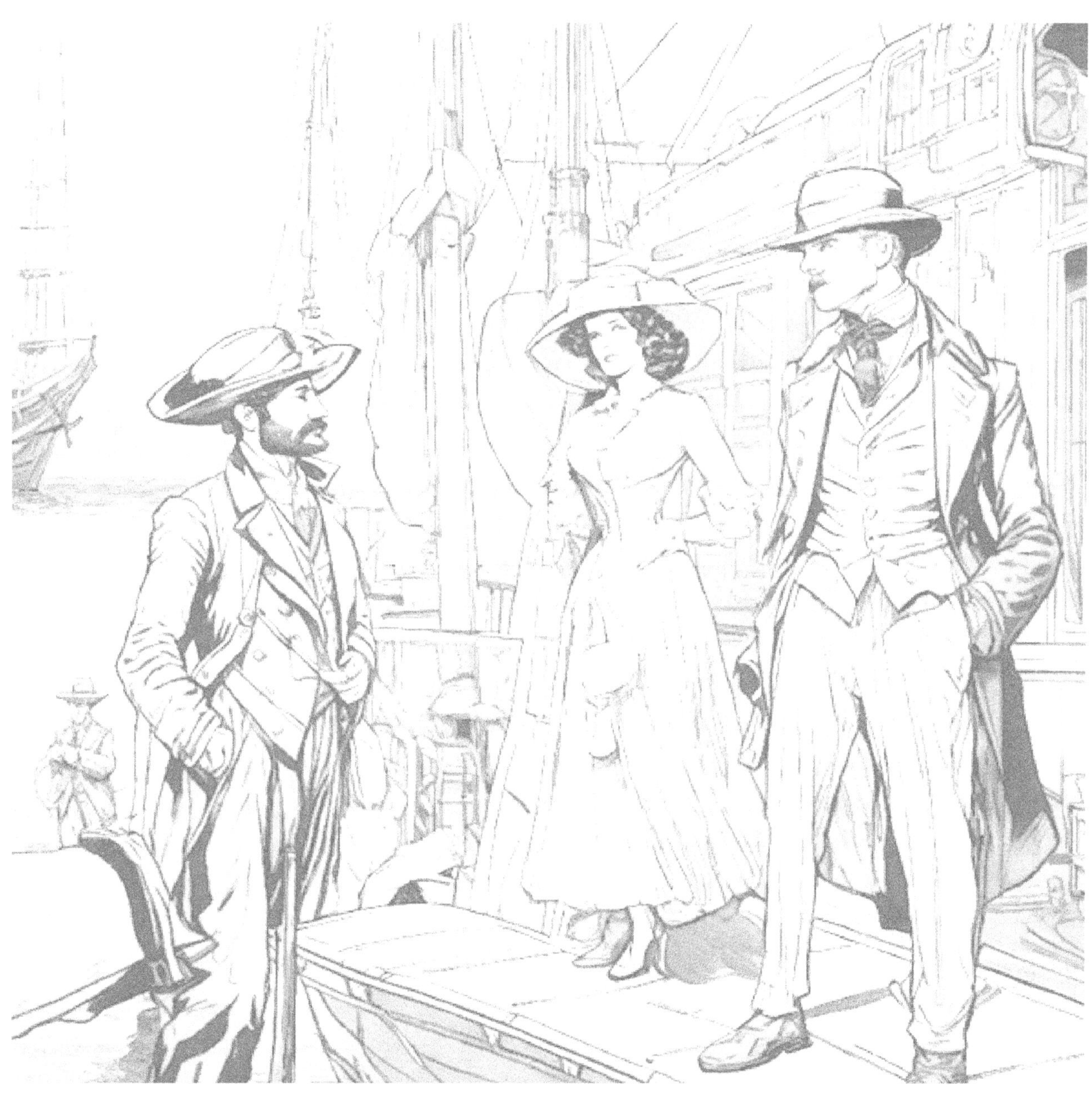

In June 1903, Sir Charles Eliot offered Lord Delamere 100,000 acres of land in Njoro, and an offer to purchase the whole area at 8d (eight pennies) per acre if he spent £500 on improvements within 5 years.

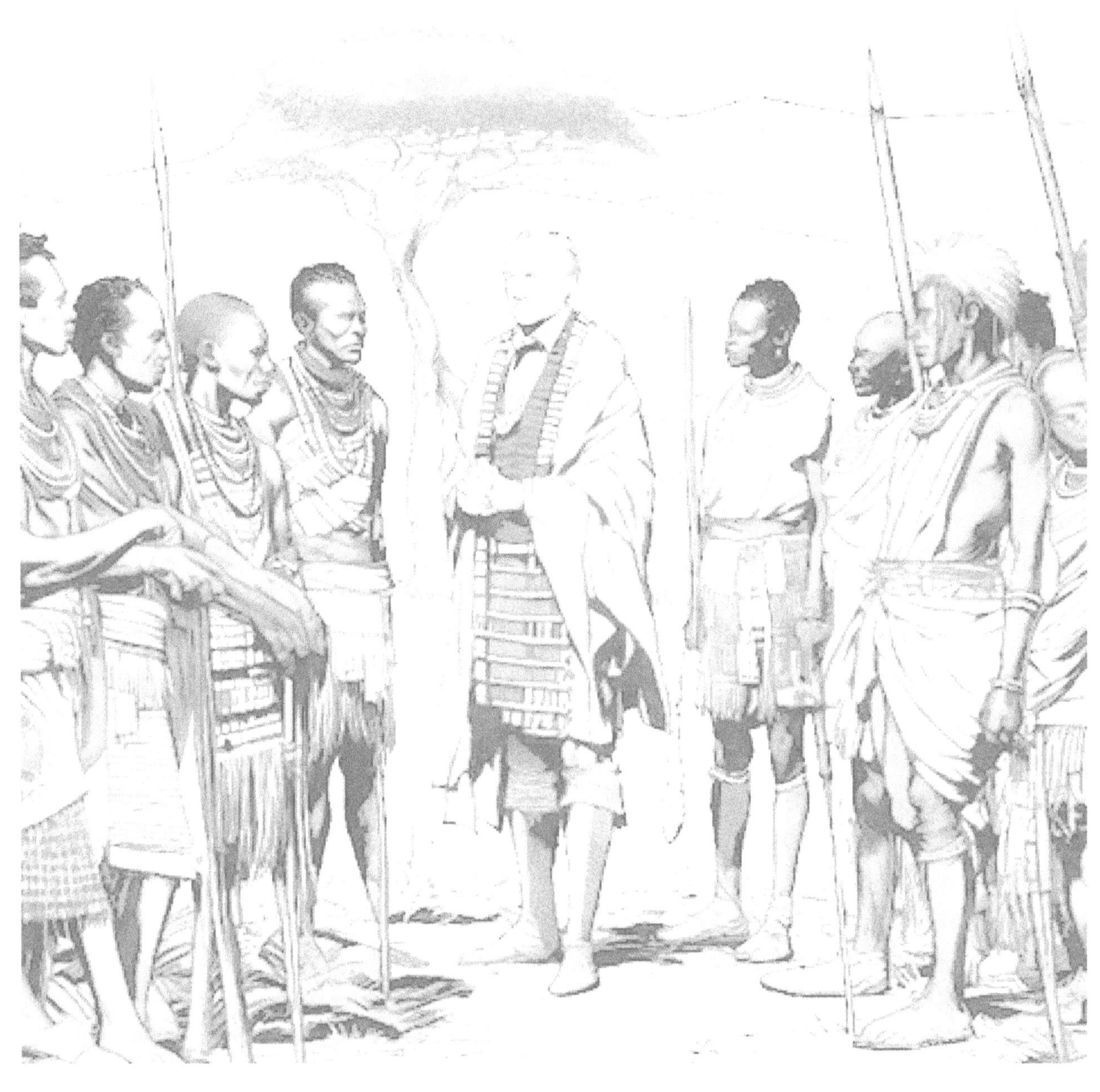

In 1904, Sir Donald William Stewart was appointed the new Commissioner and British representative to the Zanzibar Protectorate

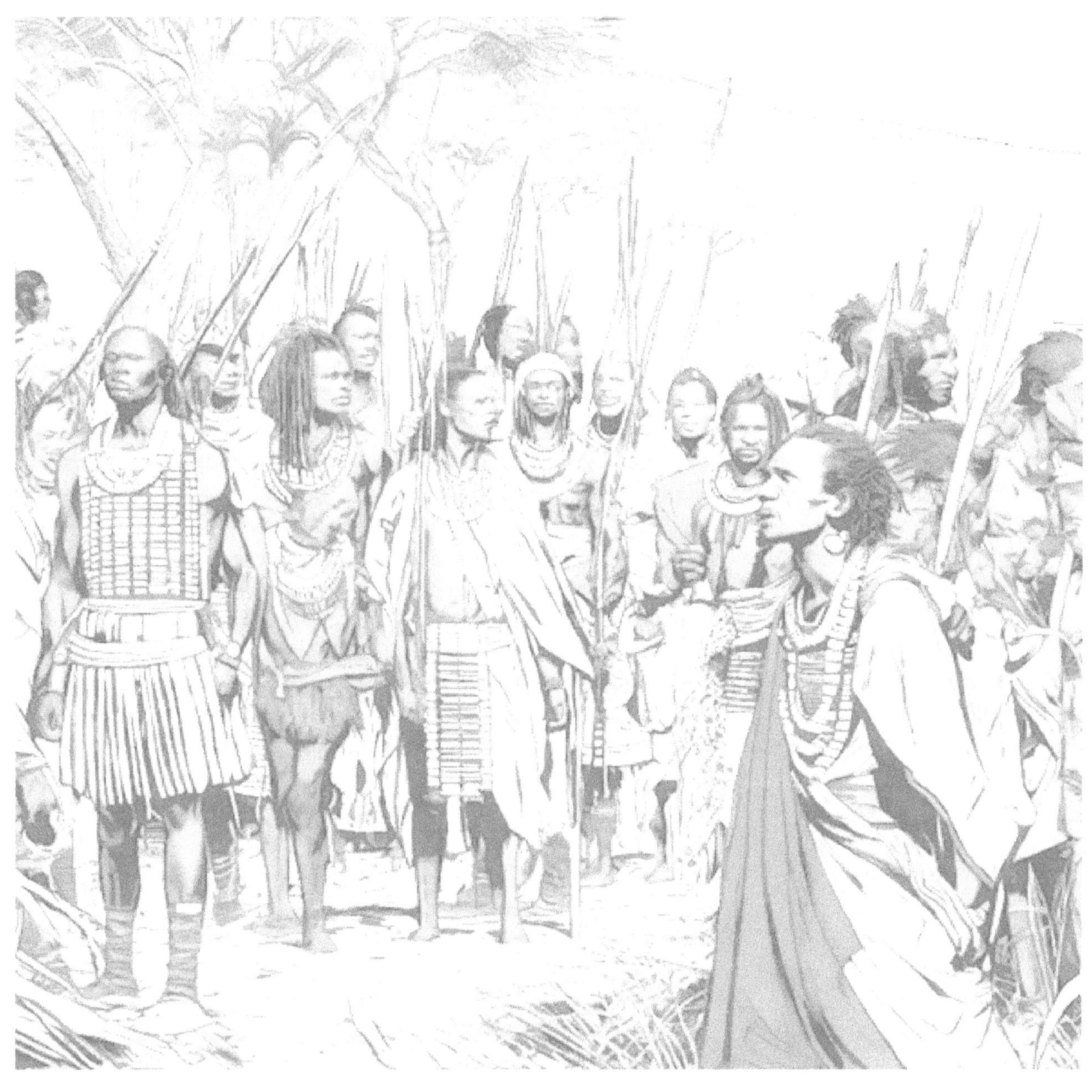

Sir Donald Stewart immediately embarked on a meeting with Maasai Elders, leading to the controversial First Anglo-Maasai Agreement and the retreat of the Maasai from parts of the Rift Valley.

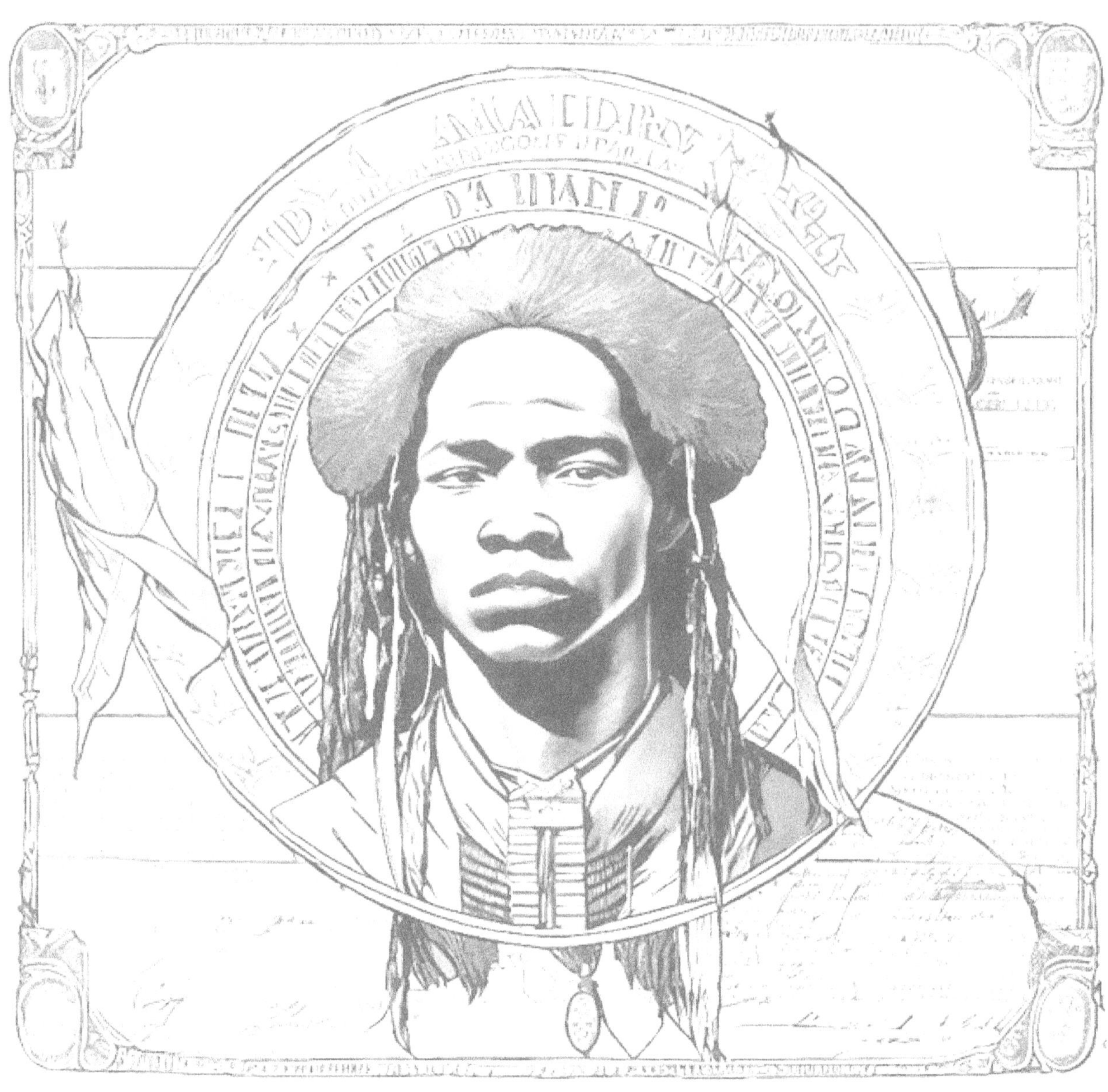

The Second Anglo- Maasai Agreement took place in 1911 and and displaced 11,000 Maasai and 22 Million cattle further South into drier lands of Kajiado and Narok.

EPISODE 5: LAND COMMITTEE

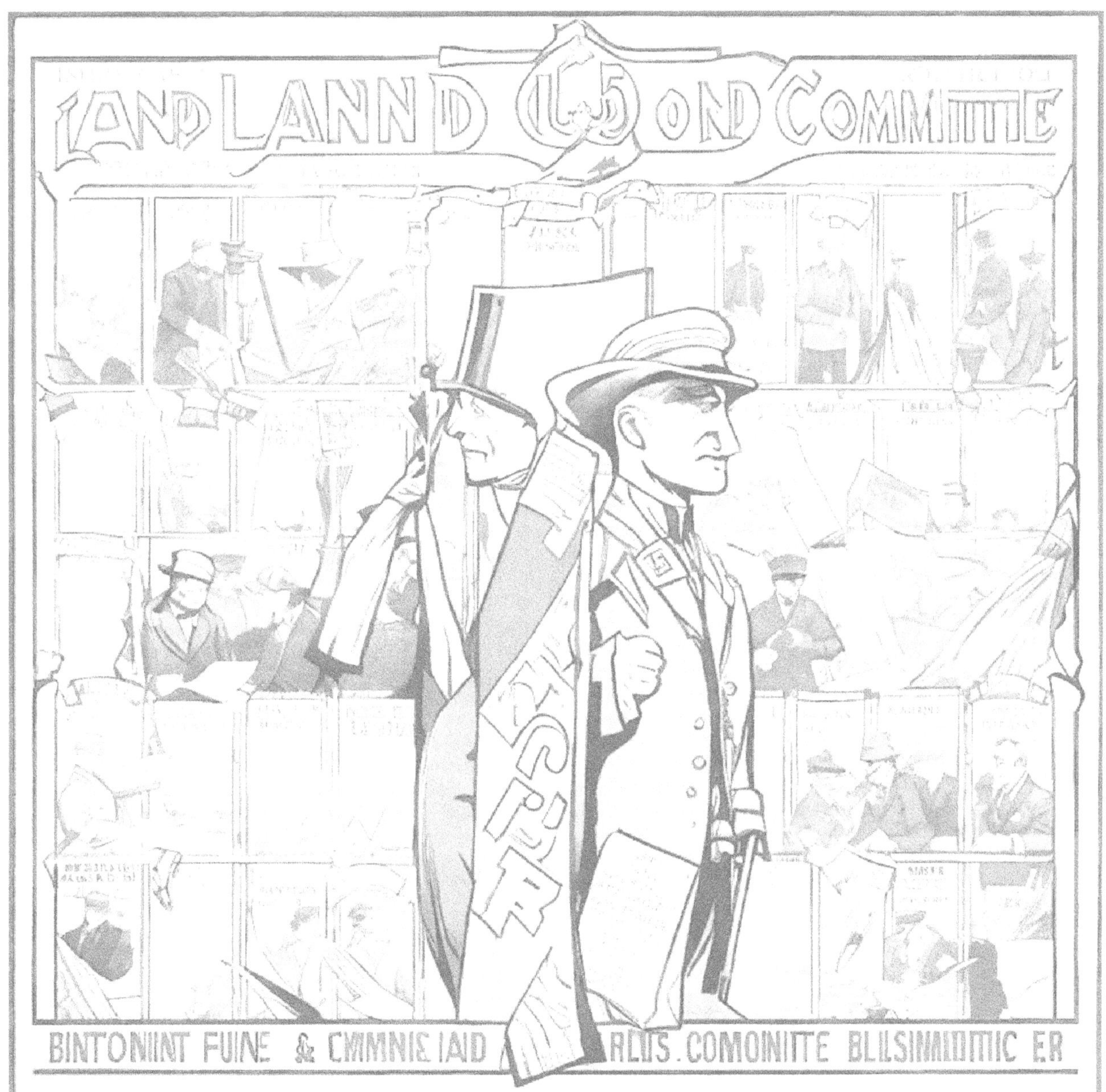

Sir Donald William Stewart empaneled a Land Committee in 1905 comprising three Judges (two later became Chief Justices) and two members of the Colonists' Association of British East Africa.

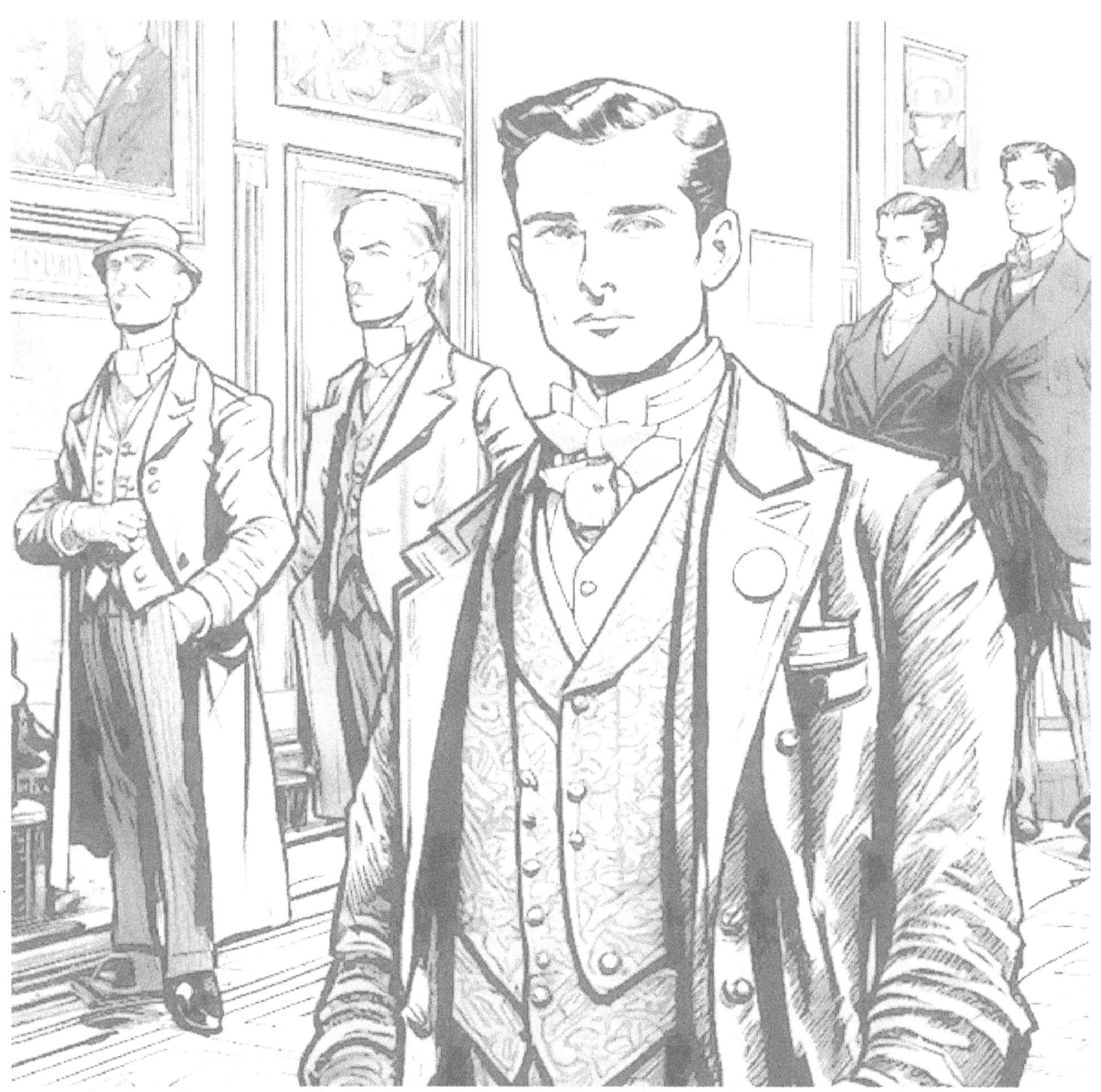

Before the Land Committee could begin its work in 1905, Judge Cator was posted to the High Court at Zanzibar and the 35 year old Lord Delamere took over as Chairman.

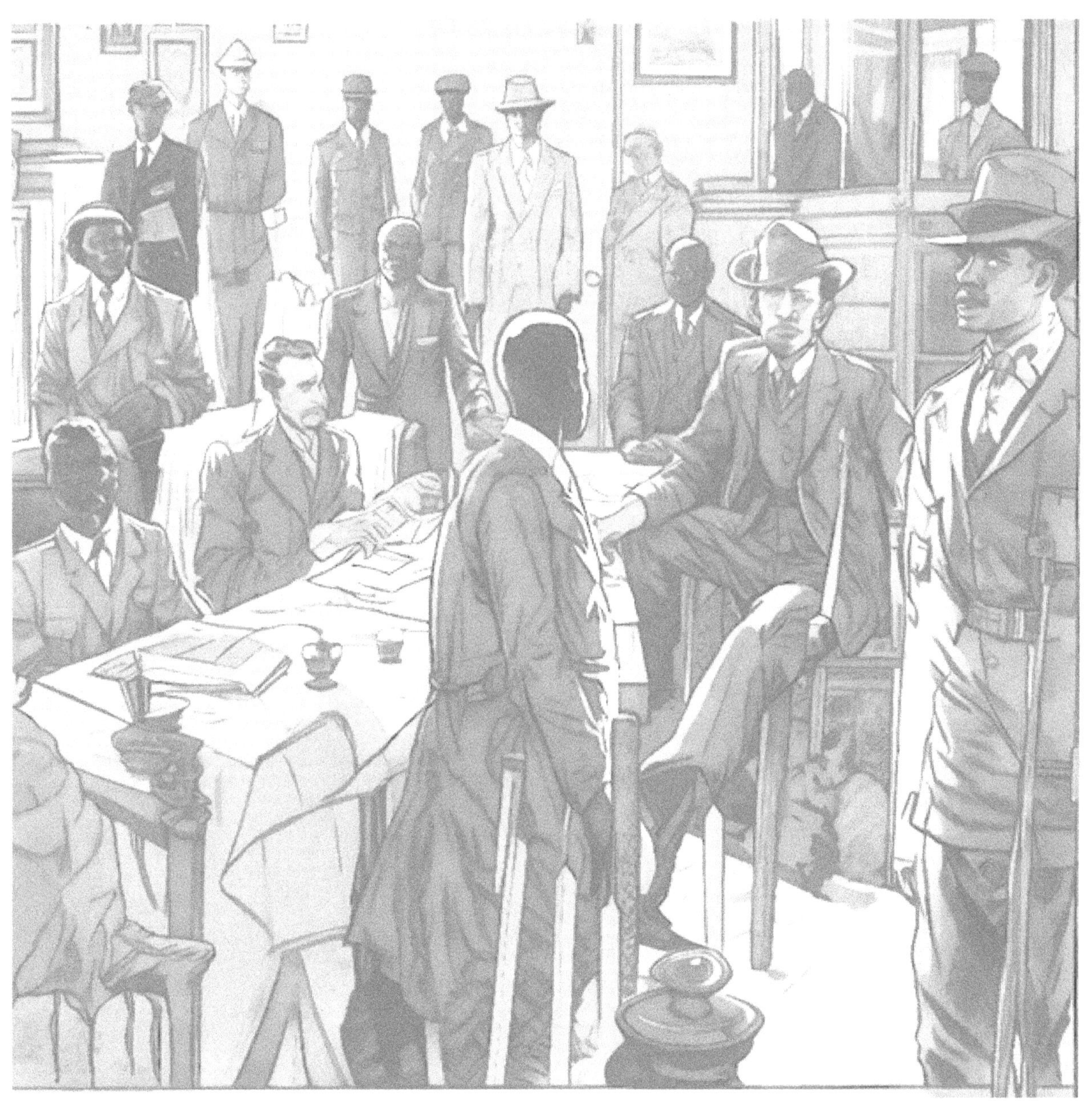

The committee held four sittings at Mombasa and fourteen in Nairobi, with 44 witnesses submitting written memoranda on issues related to land regulations and their actual administration

EPISODE 6: ZIONIST SETTLEMENT IN THE UASIN GISHU PLATEAU

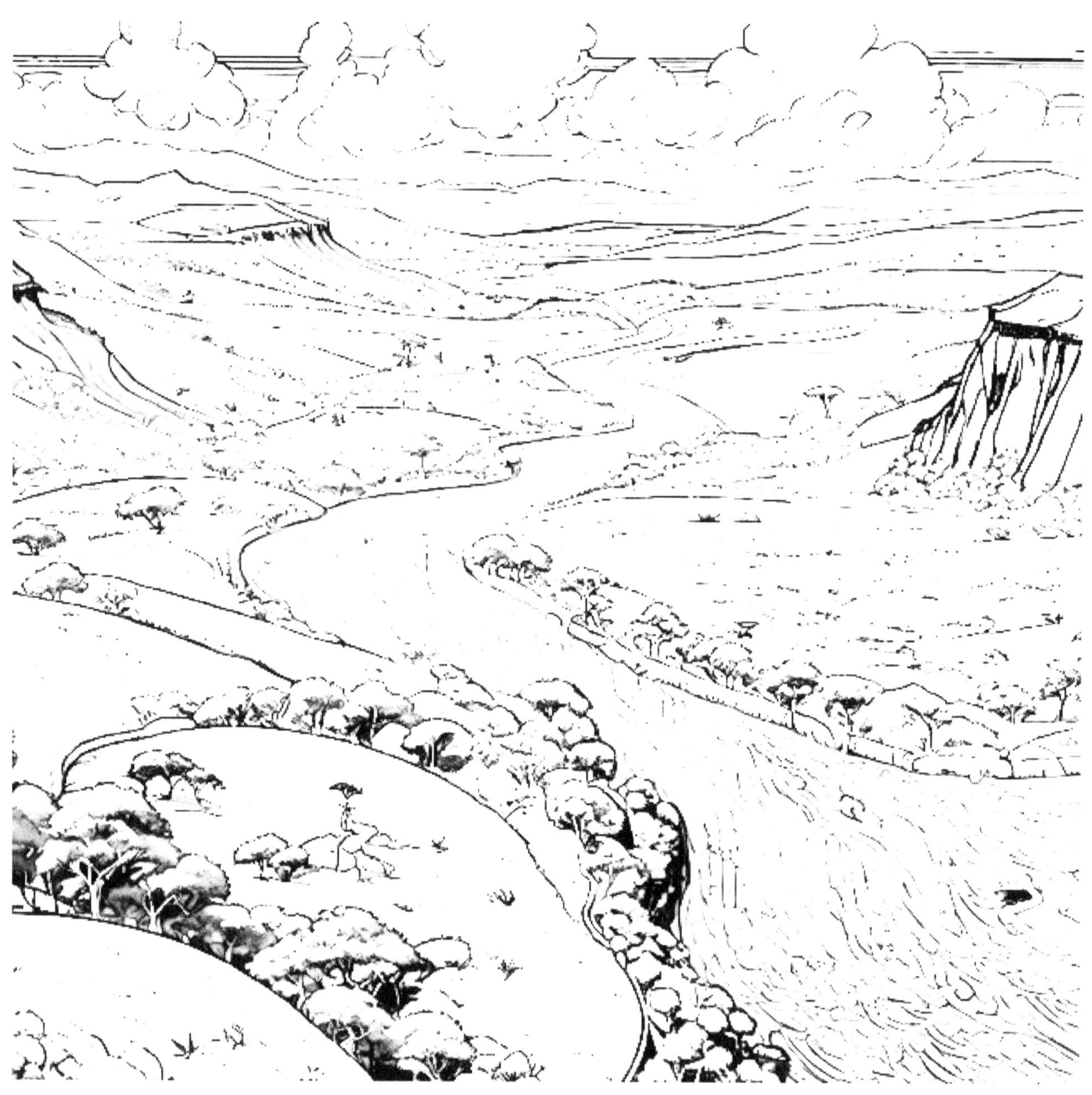

There had been an attempt to settle Finns in the East Africa Protectorate

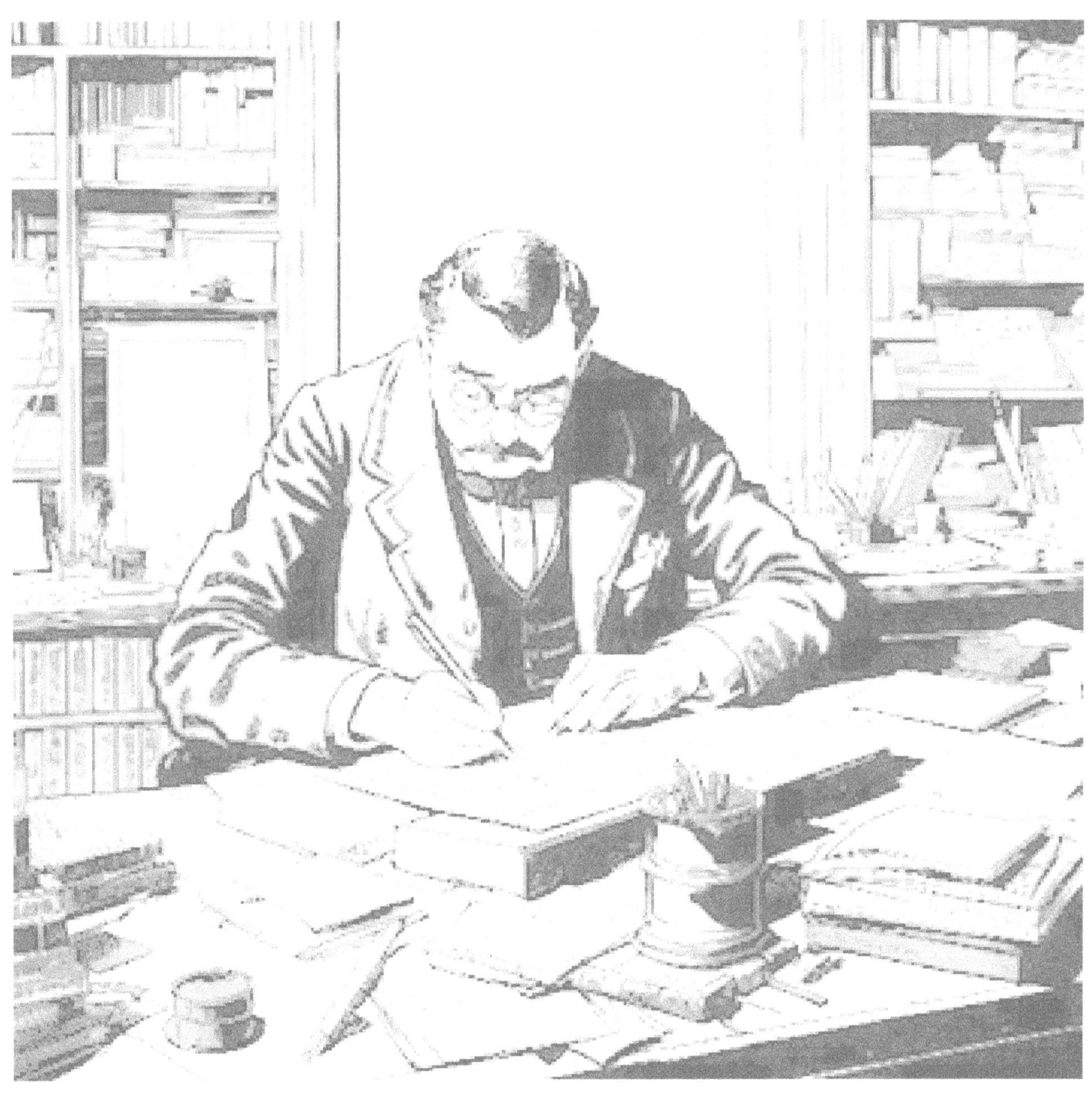

In a dispatch to Lord Lansdowne dated 11 December 1903, Sir Charles Eliot shared that owing to the Finns maritime way of life, he doubted very much whether they could succeed as agriculturalists in a tropical climate such as that of Kenya.

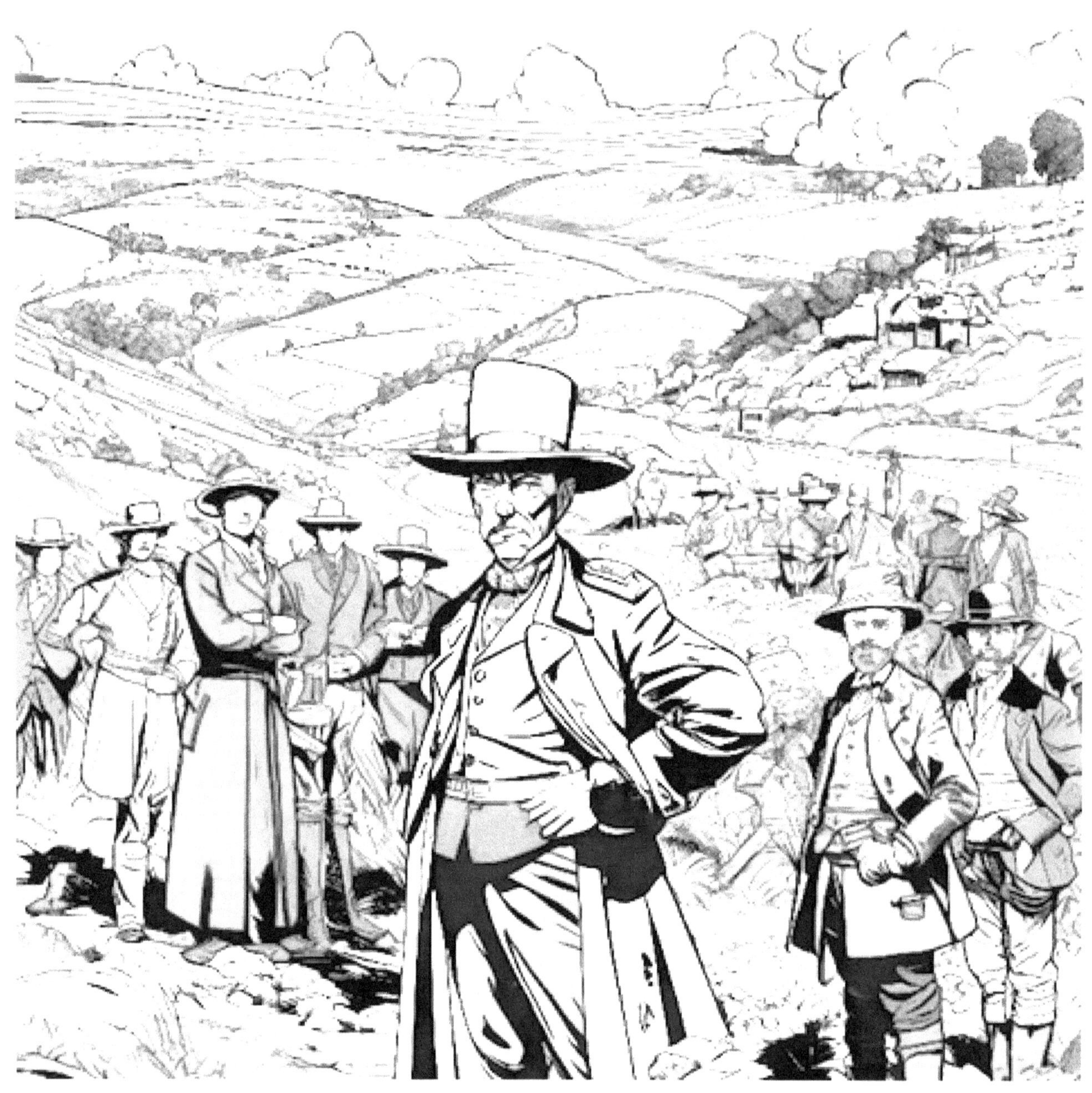

Joseph Chamberlain, the Secretary of State for the Colonies visited the East Africa Protectorate in December 1902. He was gobsmacked by the beauty of the country, the fertility of the land and of the climate.

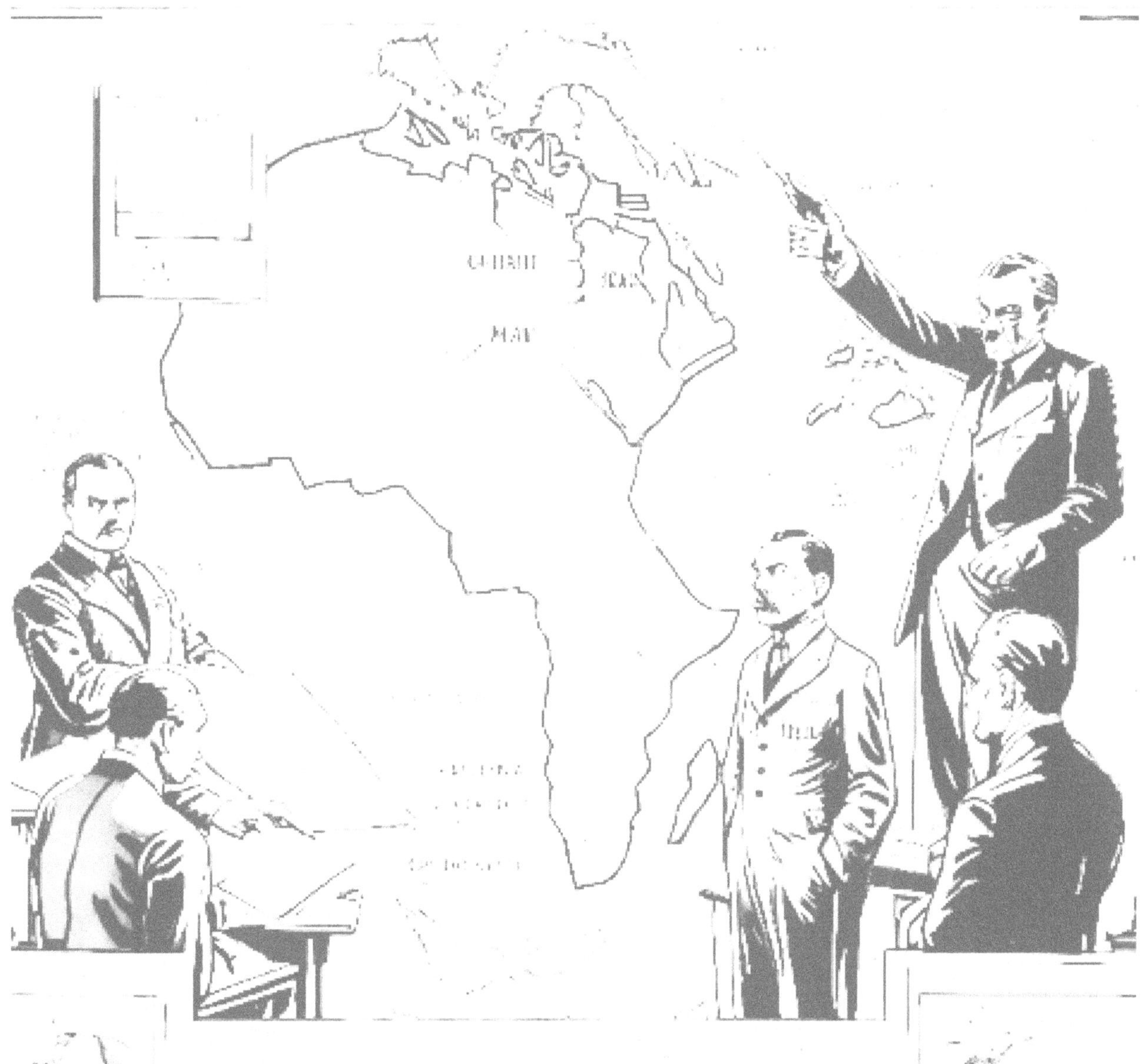

Upon return to England, Joseph Chamberlain intimated to his ministers, and key officials in his department his plans to settle Jews in the Uasin Gishu Plateau

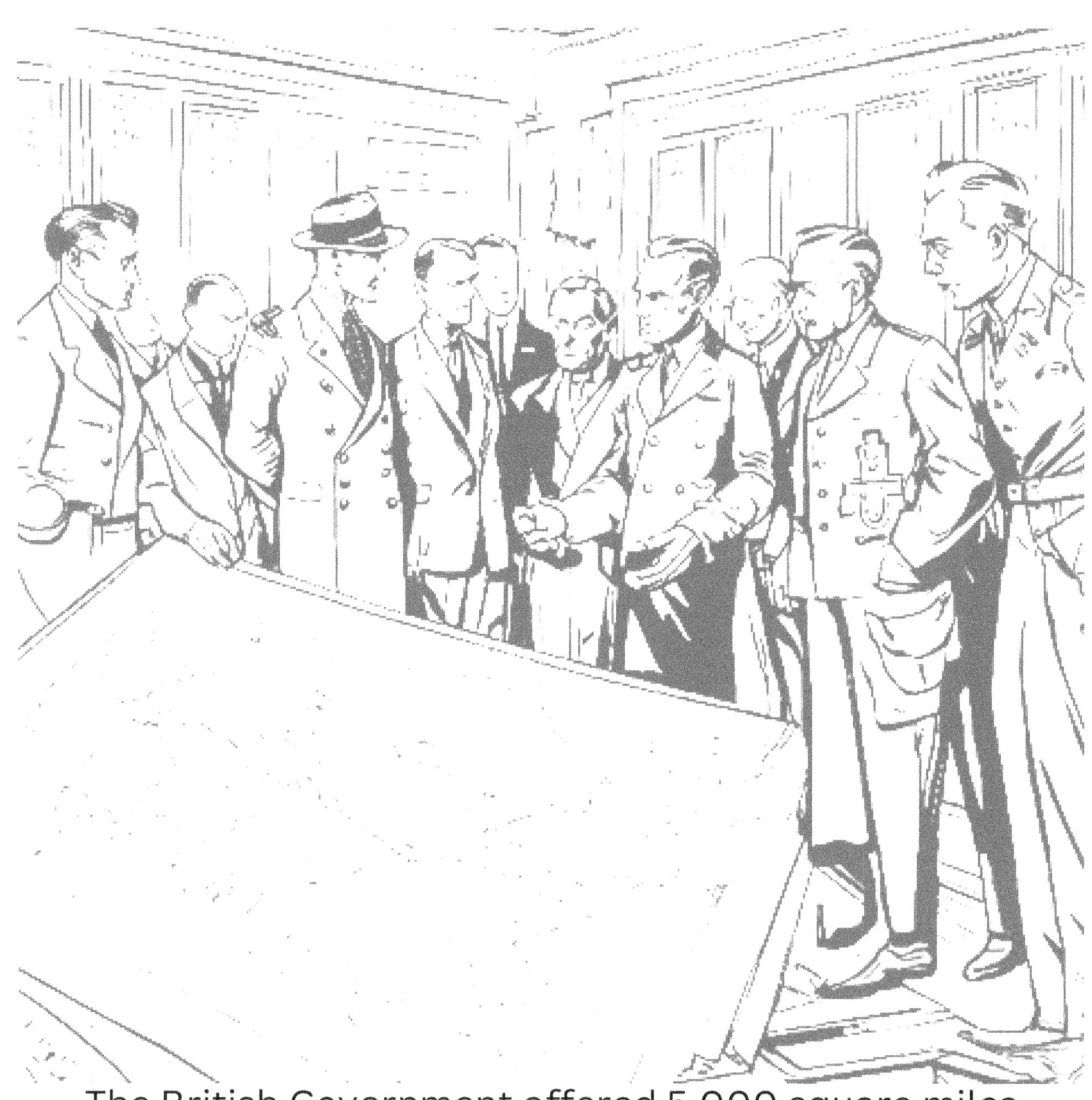

The British Government offered 5,000 square miles (3,200,000 acres) in the Uasin Gishu Plateau on free grant as a new homeland for European Jews.

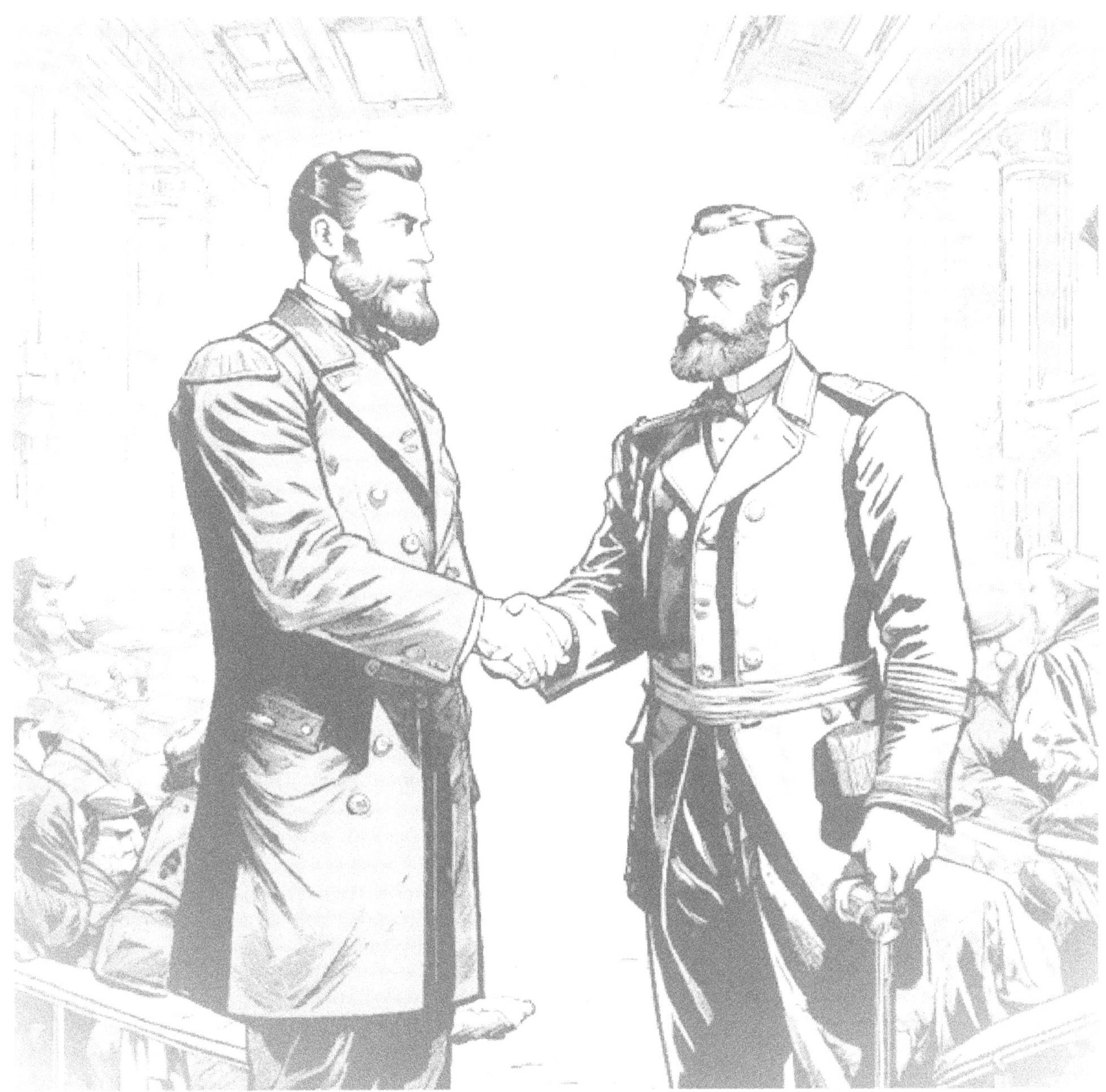

Theodor Herzl and other Zionist leaders in England accepted the offer as an "ante-chamber to the Holy Land".

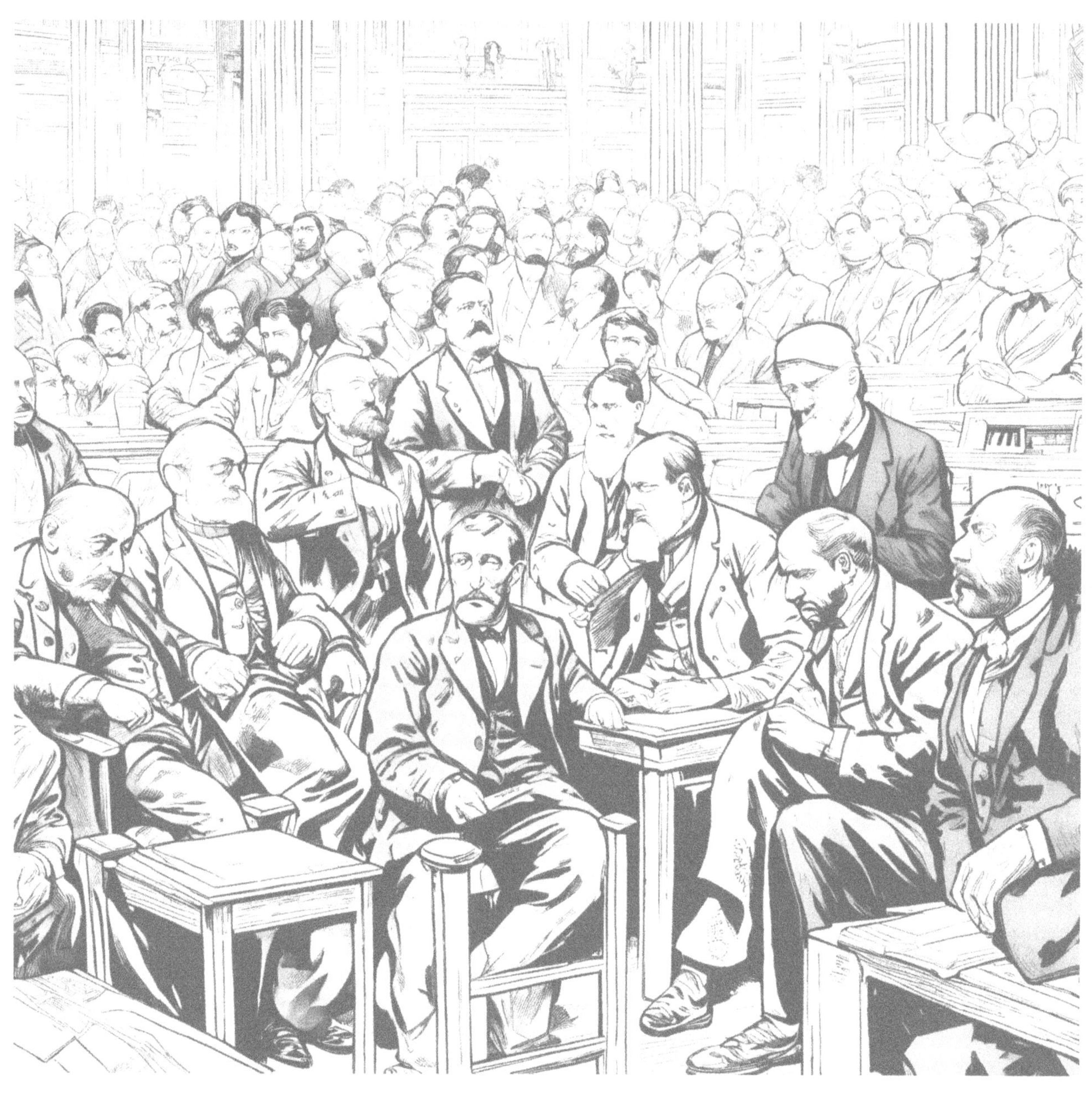

When word reached the settlers in the East Africa Protectorate, they were incensed, first at what they perceived as betrayal by Joseph Chamberlain, and then at the prospects of sharing prestigious highlands.

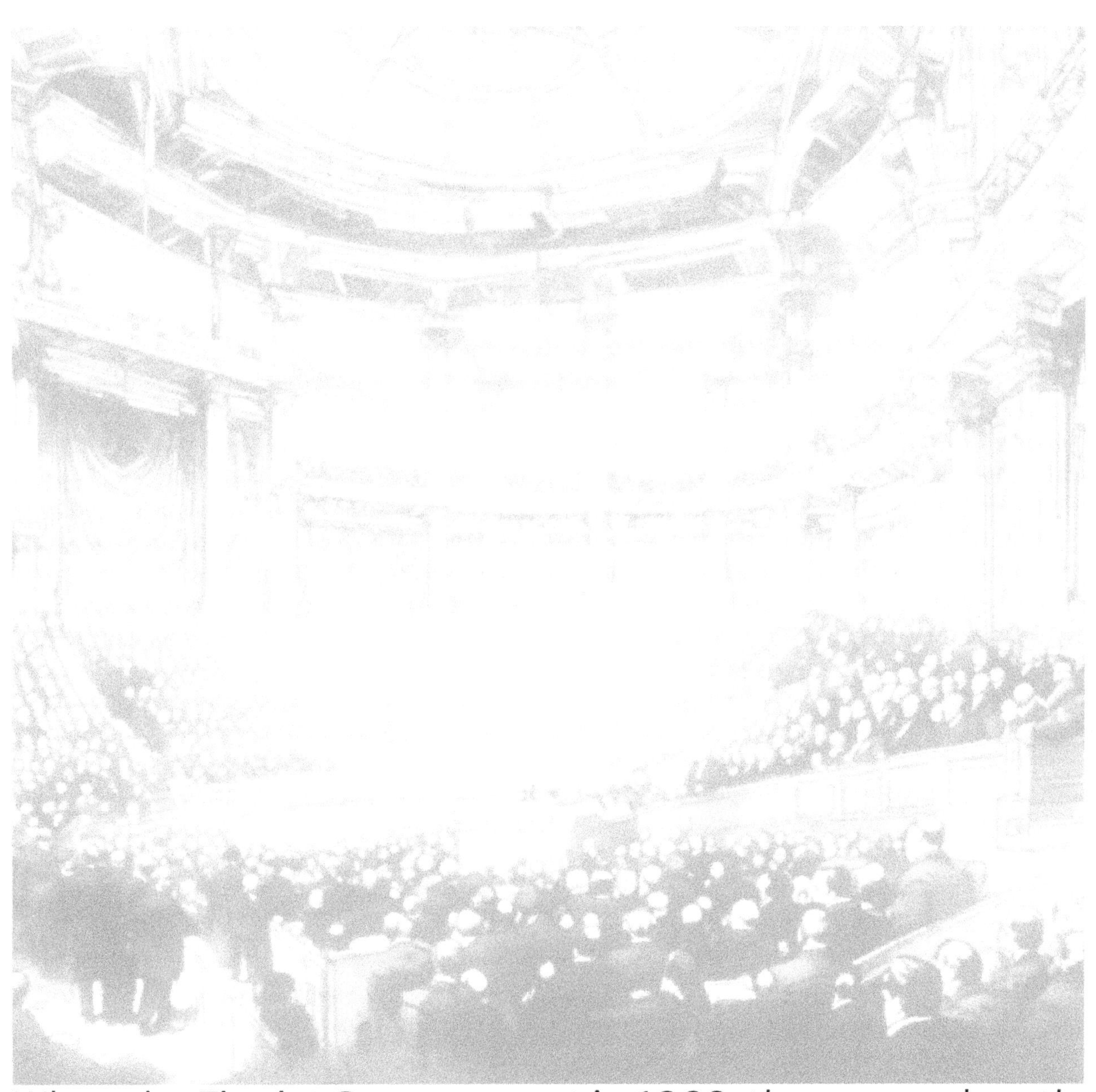

When the Zionist Congress met in 1903, there was a lengthy debate on the Uasin Gishu settlement.

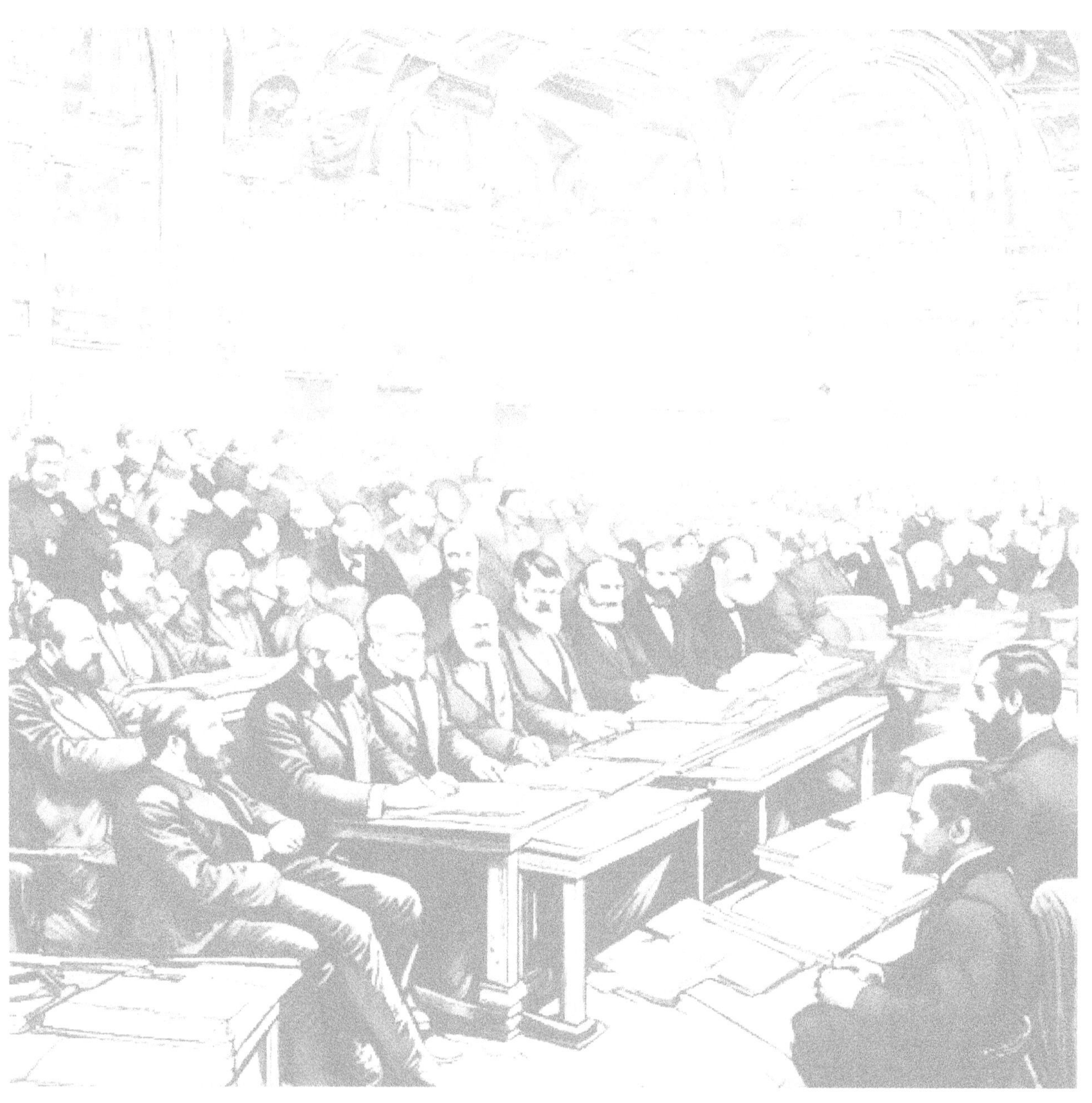

The Russian Jews and delegates from Bessarabia rejected
the offer

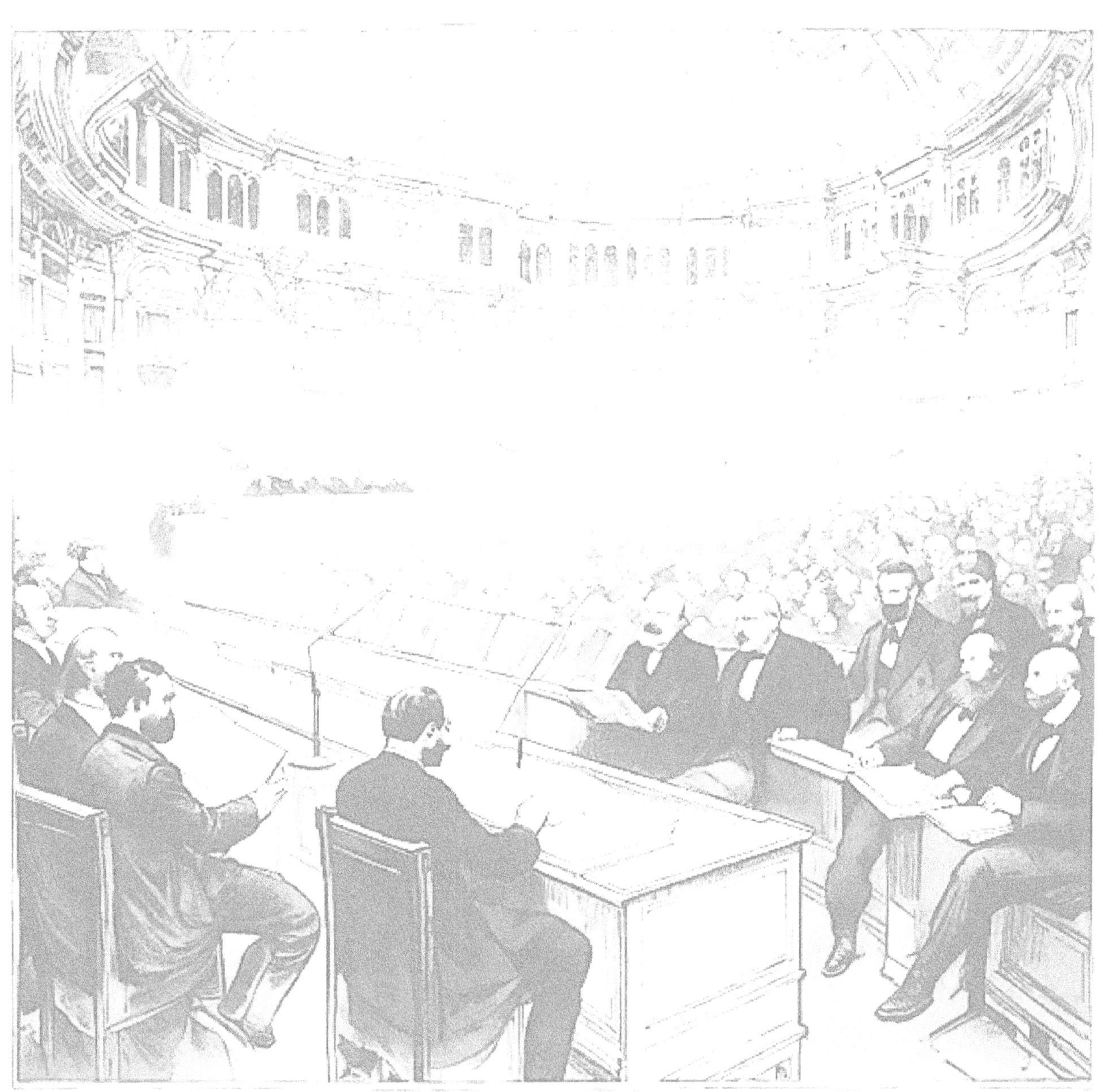

A 295 to 177 vote to send a committee of investigators to the East Africa Protectorate and to report on the suitability of establishing a national home for European Jews there.

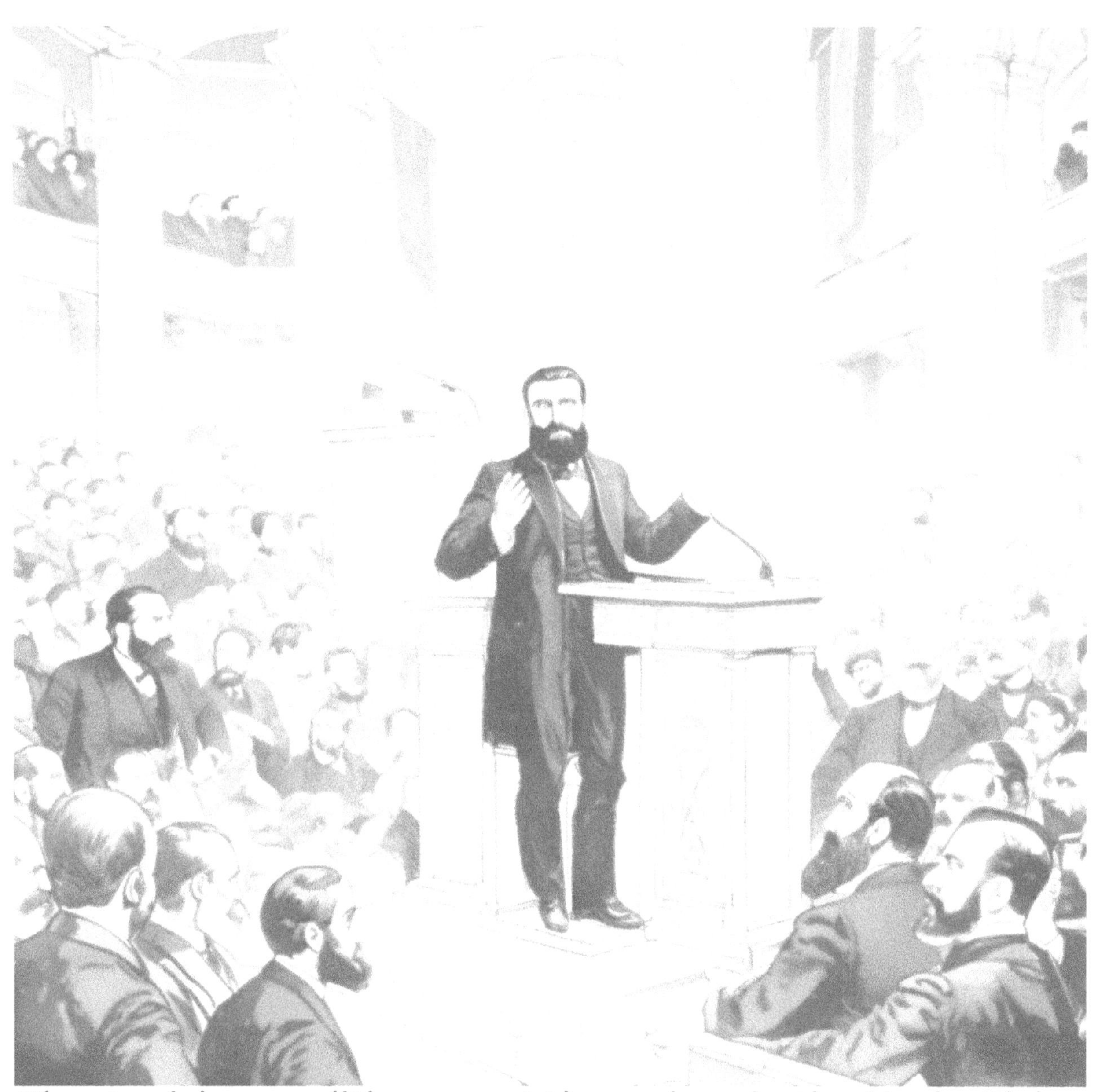

The Jewish expedition spent three days in the Uasin Gishu plateau and submitted their report to the Seventh Zionist Congress held from 27 July to 2 August 1905.

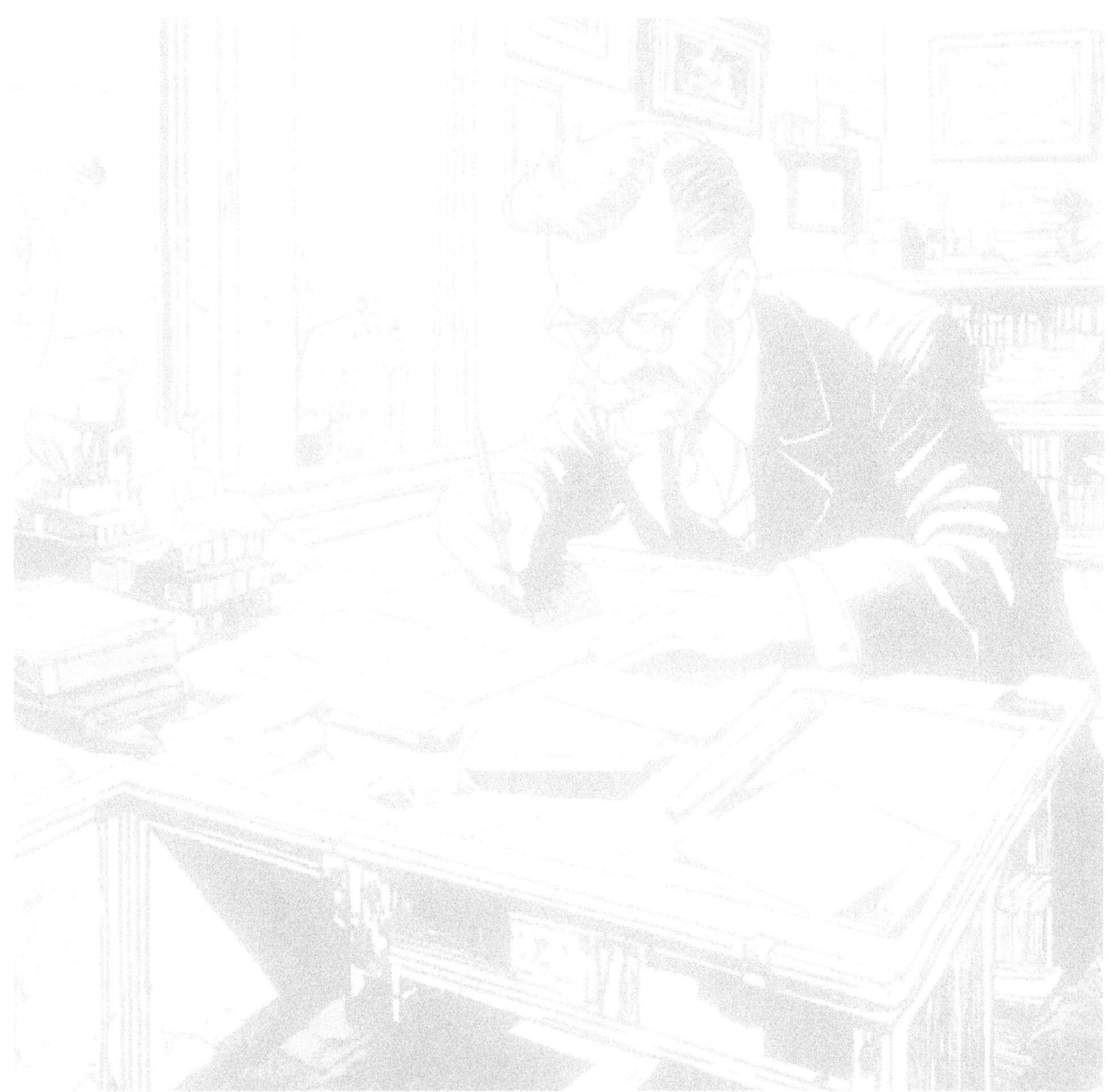

A communique to the British Government from Leopold Jacob Greenberg, the editor of The Jewish Chronicle stated that due to unfavourable reports from the members of the expedition, it was resolved to forego the whole idea

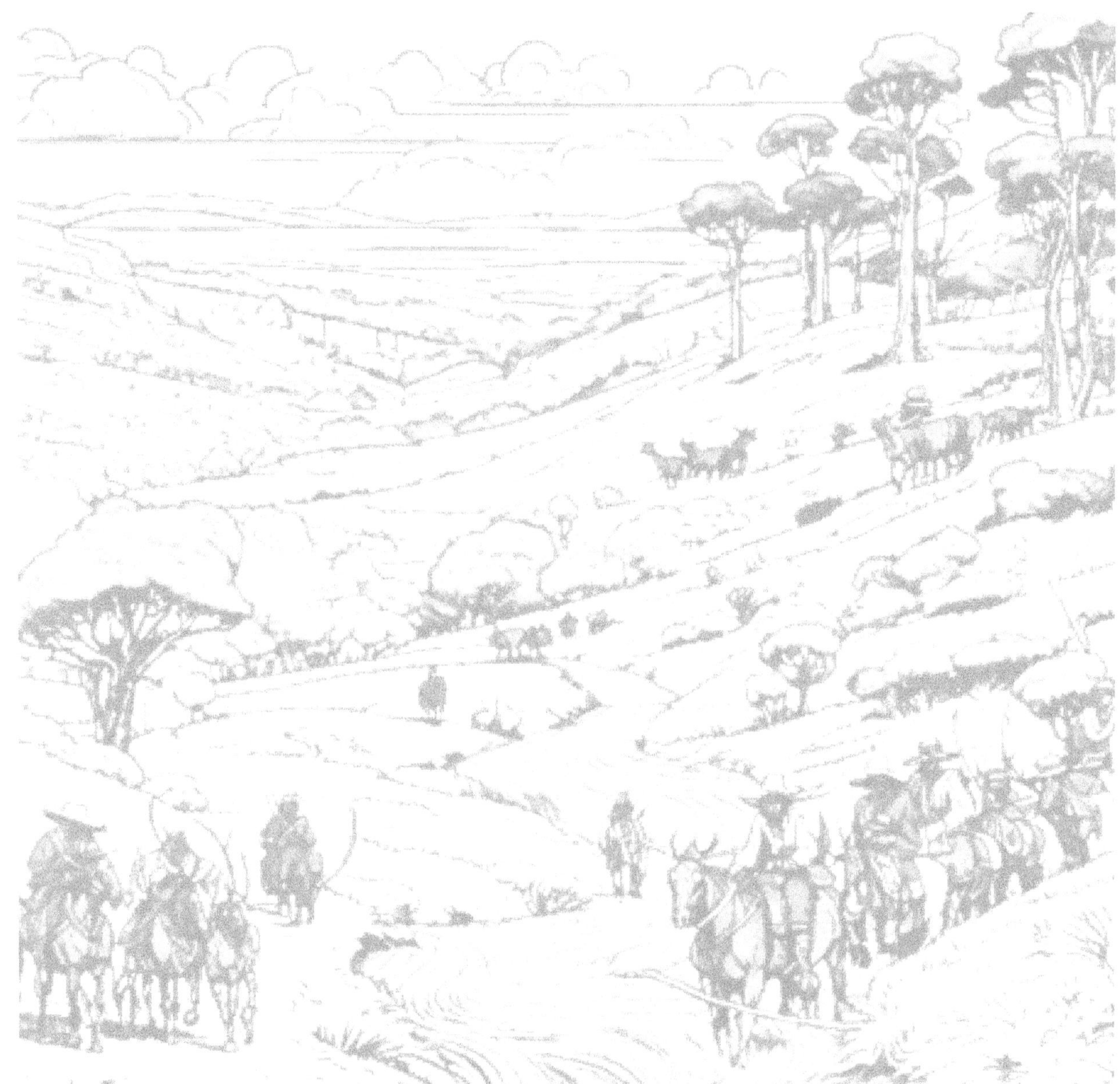

Boers, who trekked from Mombasa to the Uasin Gishu plateau, described it as a paradise whose climate resembled that of the South African Highveld region

EPISODE 7: HOLA CAMP

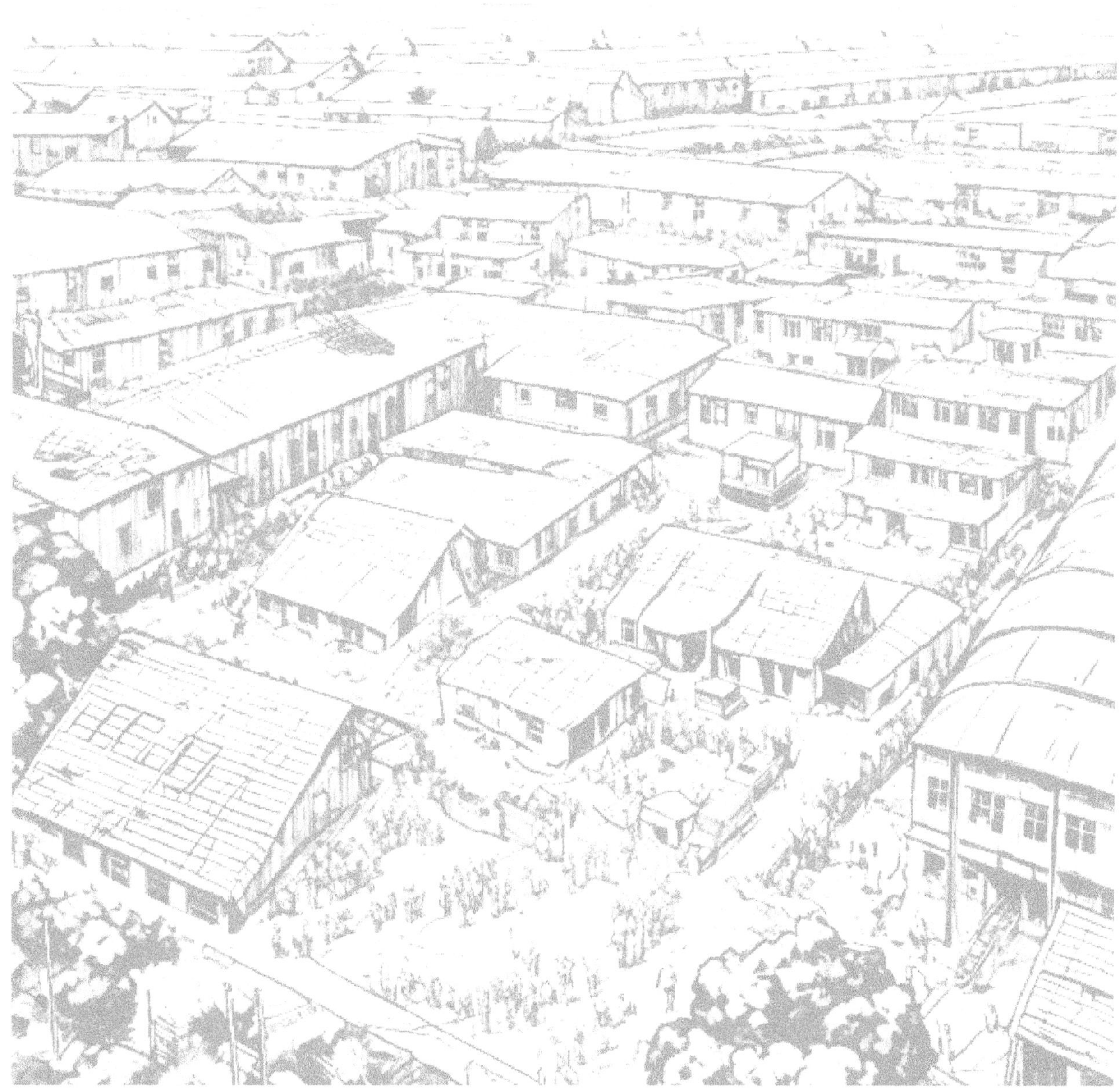

Hola Camp, had been established to house "hard-core" detainees during the Mau Mau agitation for freedom from colonial rule.

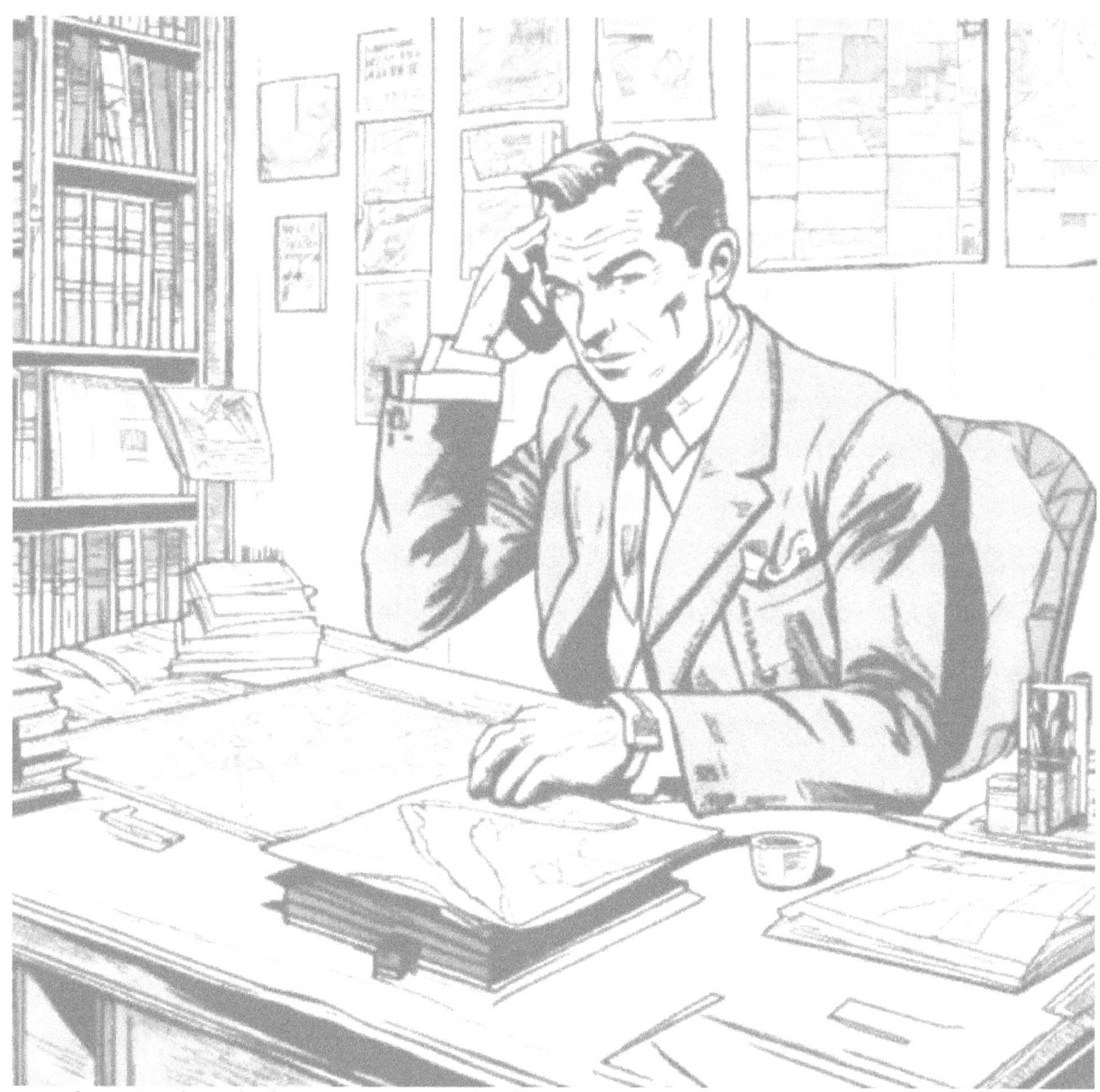

The Colonial Governor informed the Colonial Secretary that 11 inmates who died at the Hola detention camp in March 1959 were beaten to death

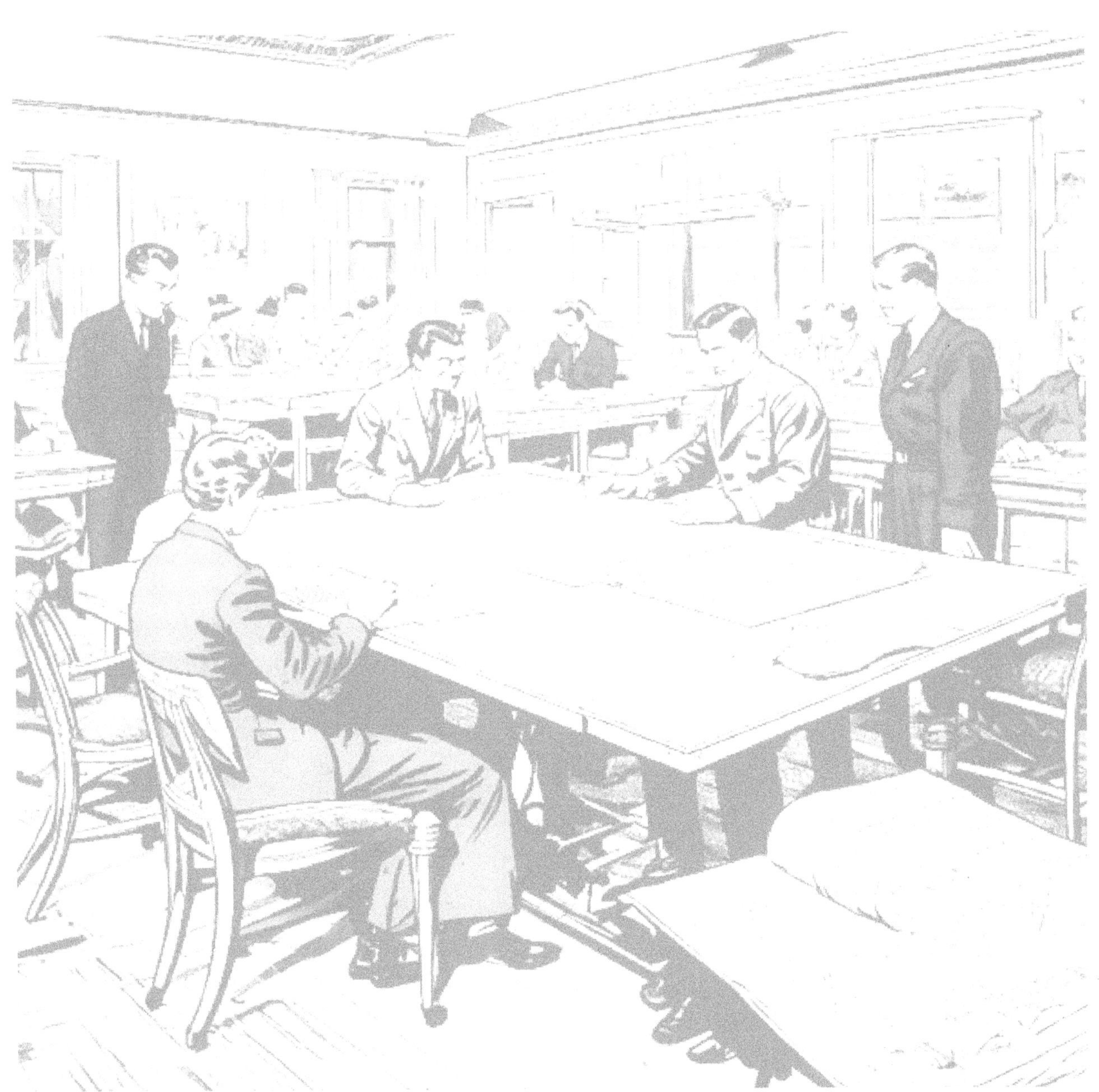

The Colonial Office had prescribed Multi-racialism as a constitutional order with the predominant roles for settlers in both the executive and legislature, while the least influential roles went to the African majority.

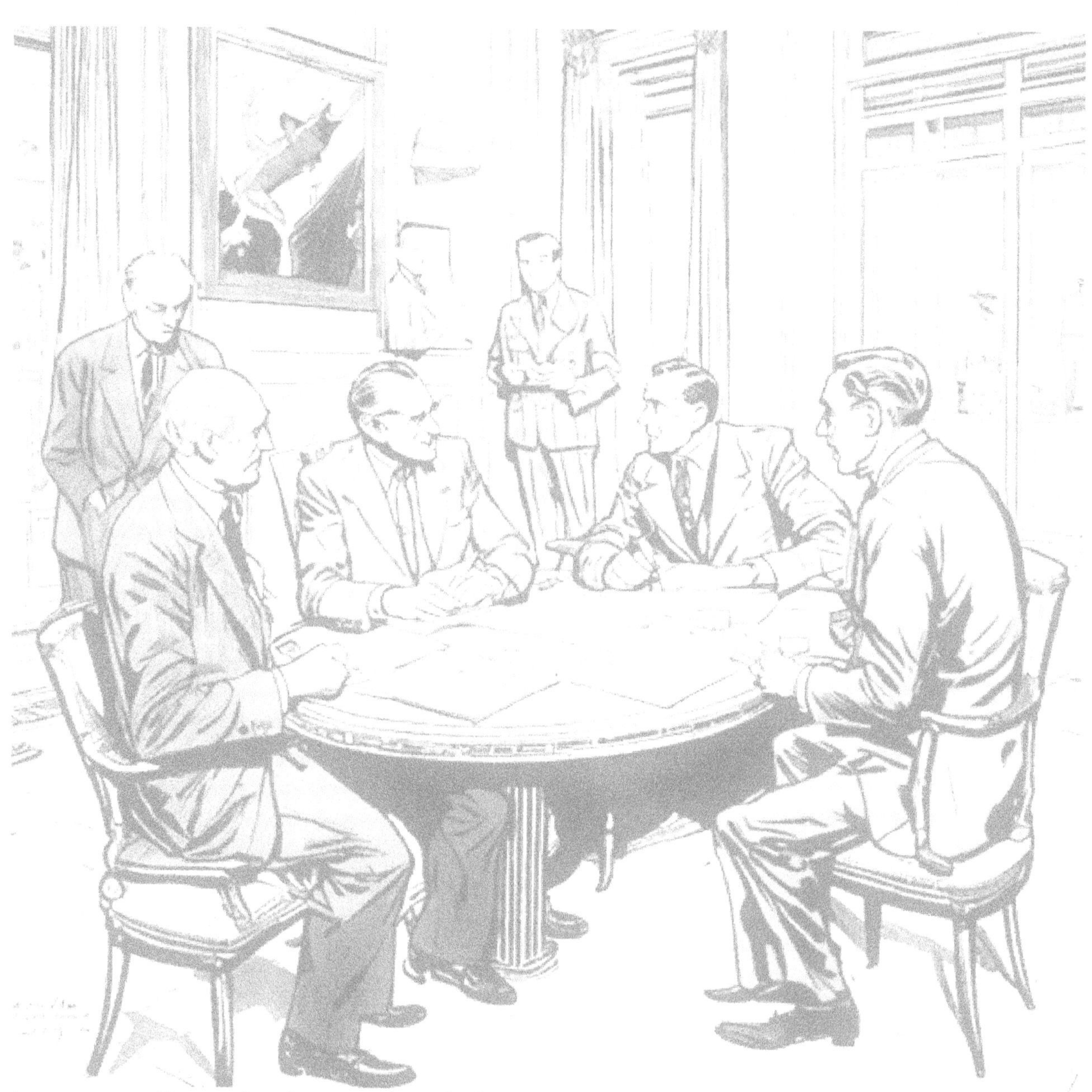

Lennox-Boyd, the Colonial Secretary and Sir Evelyn Baring, Kenya's Colonial Governor, entrusted Sir Michael Blundell, then Minister for Agriculture with the duty of building multiracial support.

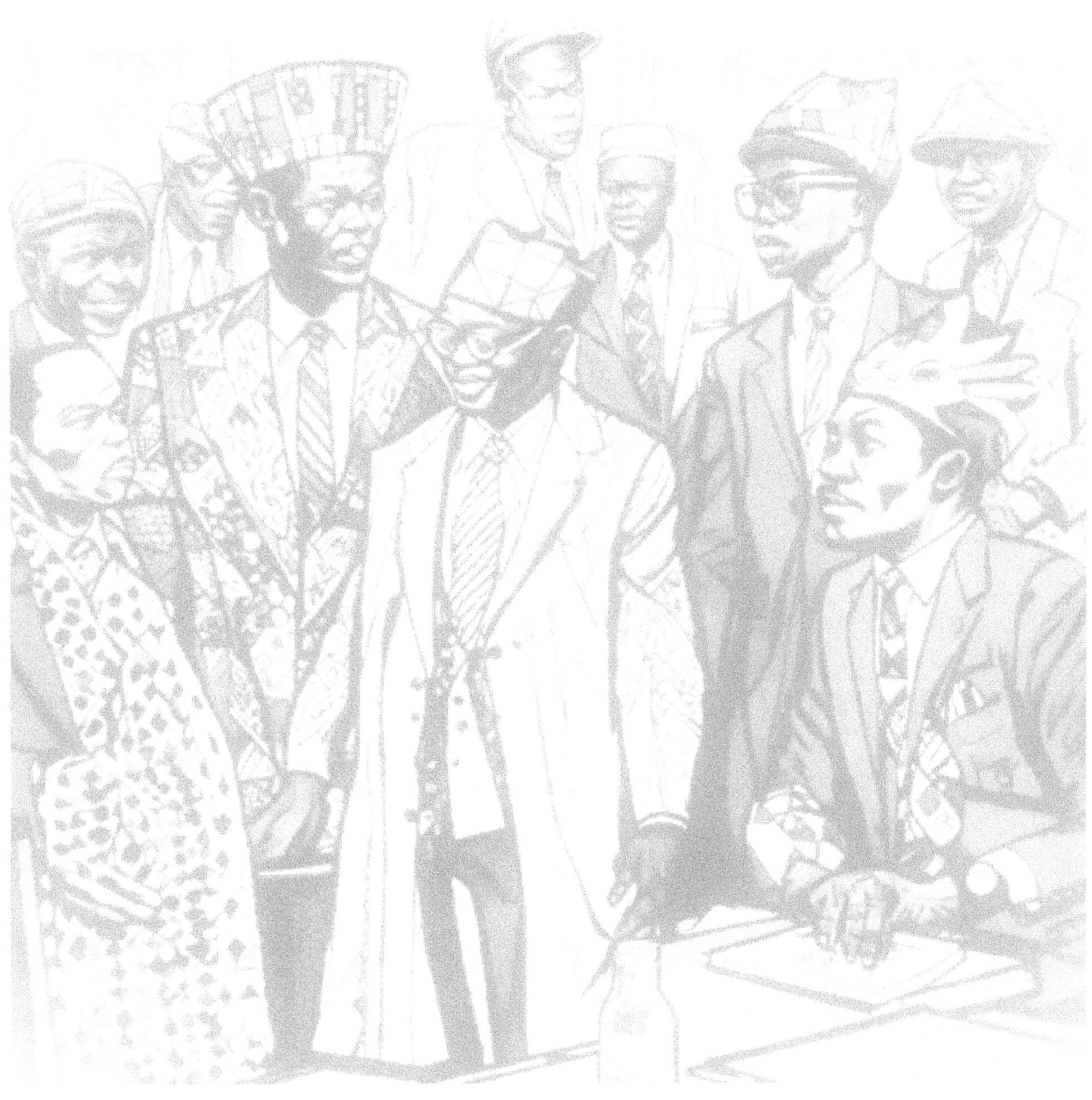

In January 1960, leading Kenyan politicians were invited to a Conference in London. Independence was beckoning faster than any of them expected.

EPISODE 8: CONSTITUTIONAL ACROBATICS

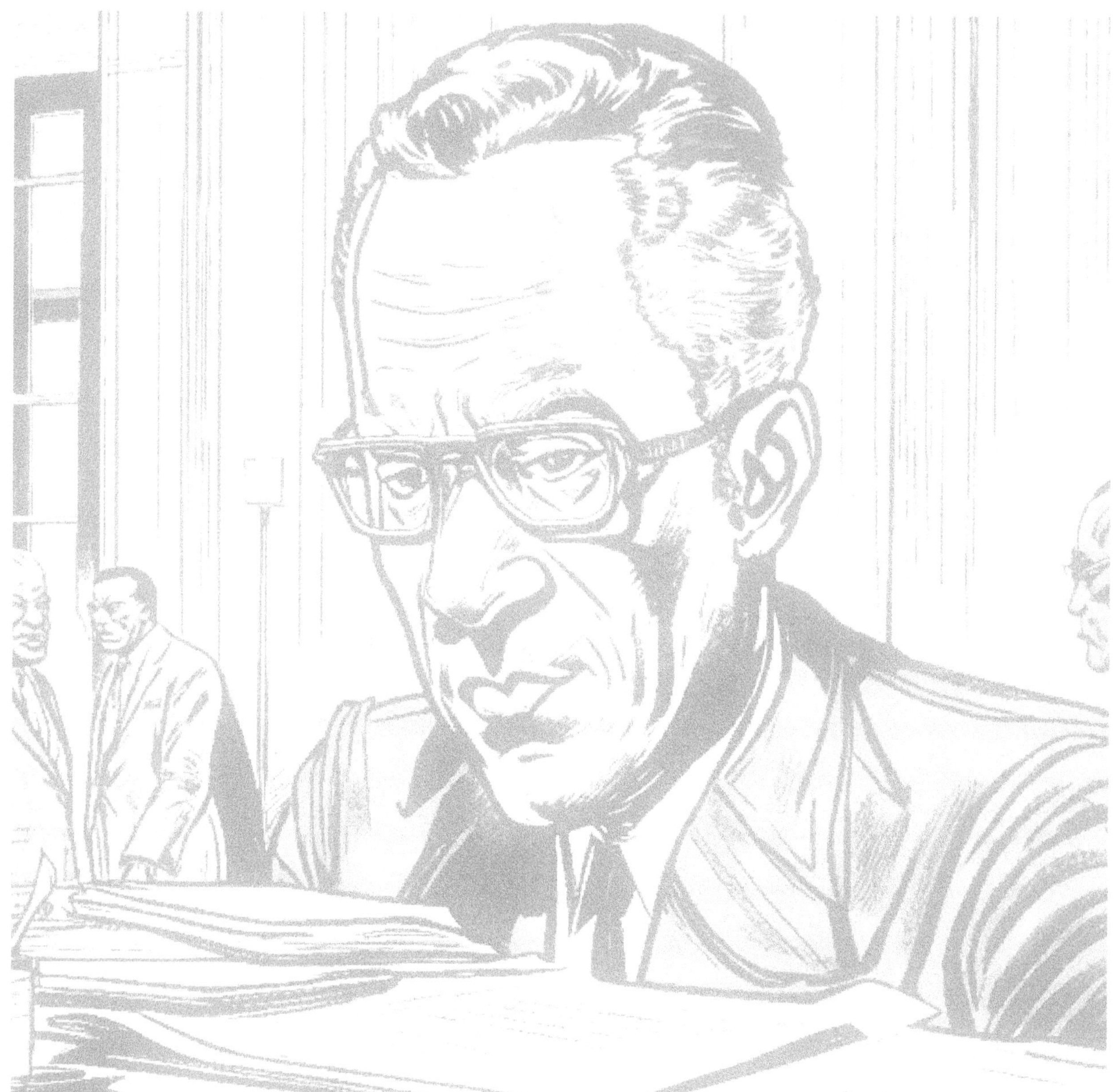

Thurgood Marshall of the National Association for the Advancement of Colored People (NAACP) was invited to the independence conference as Adviser for the united African front

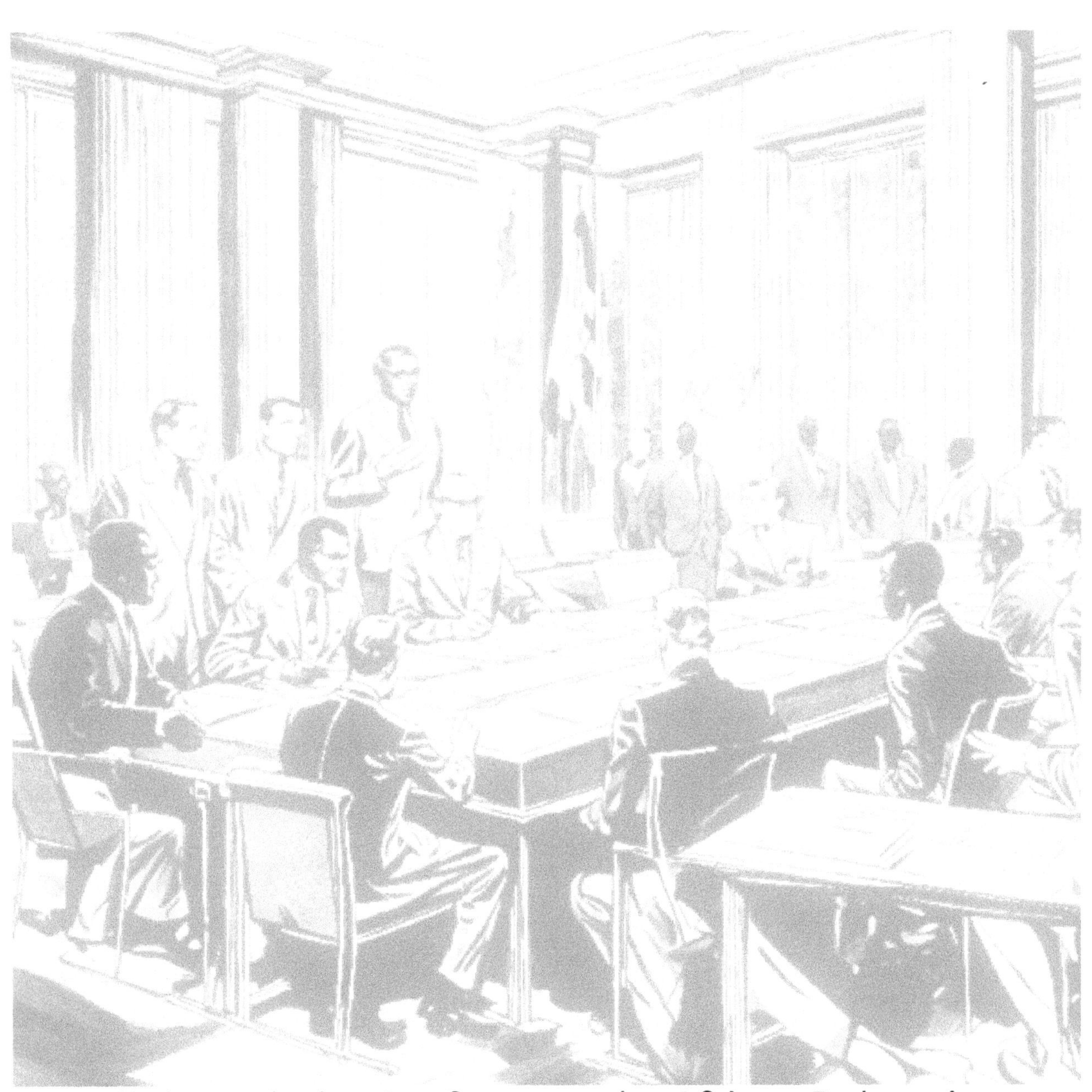

All through the Conference, the African Delegation demanded for an independence timetable and the determination of land rights.

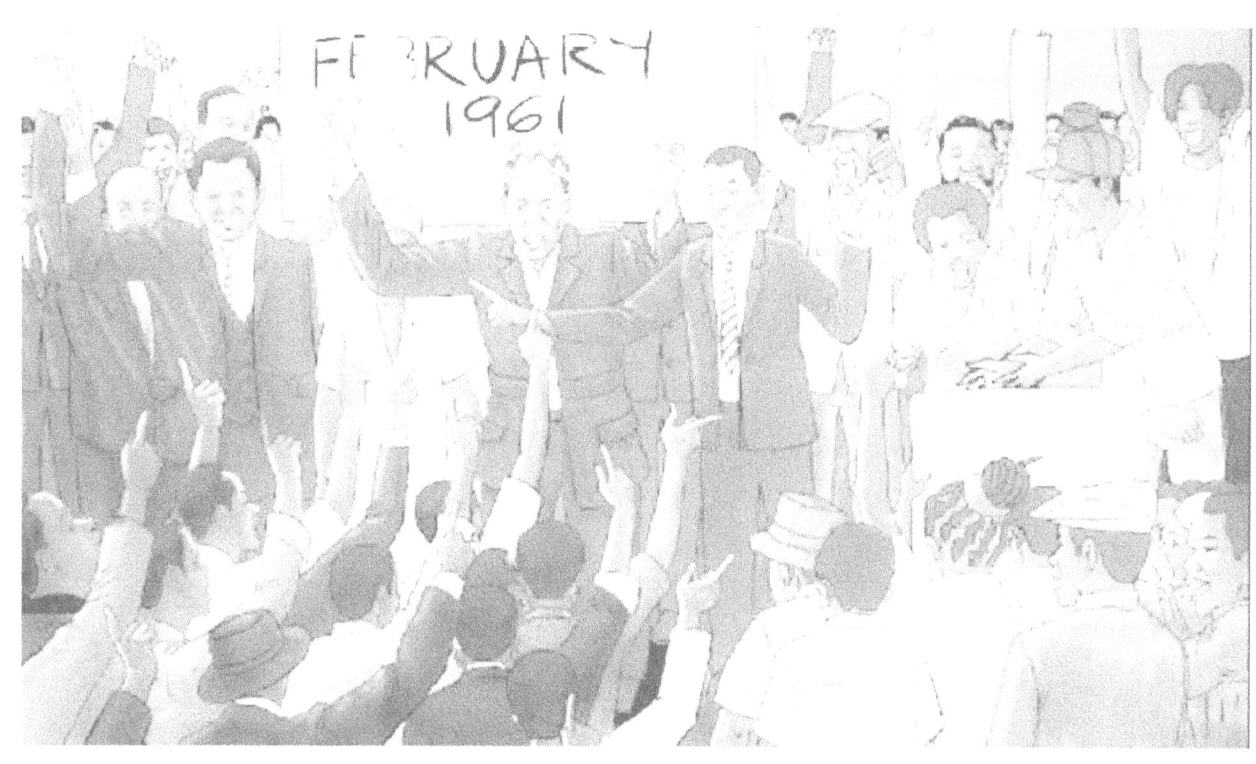

On 27 February 1961, the Kenya African Union (KANU) won 19 of the 53 common roll seats. The Kenya African Democratic Union (KADU) got 12 seats

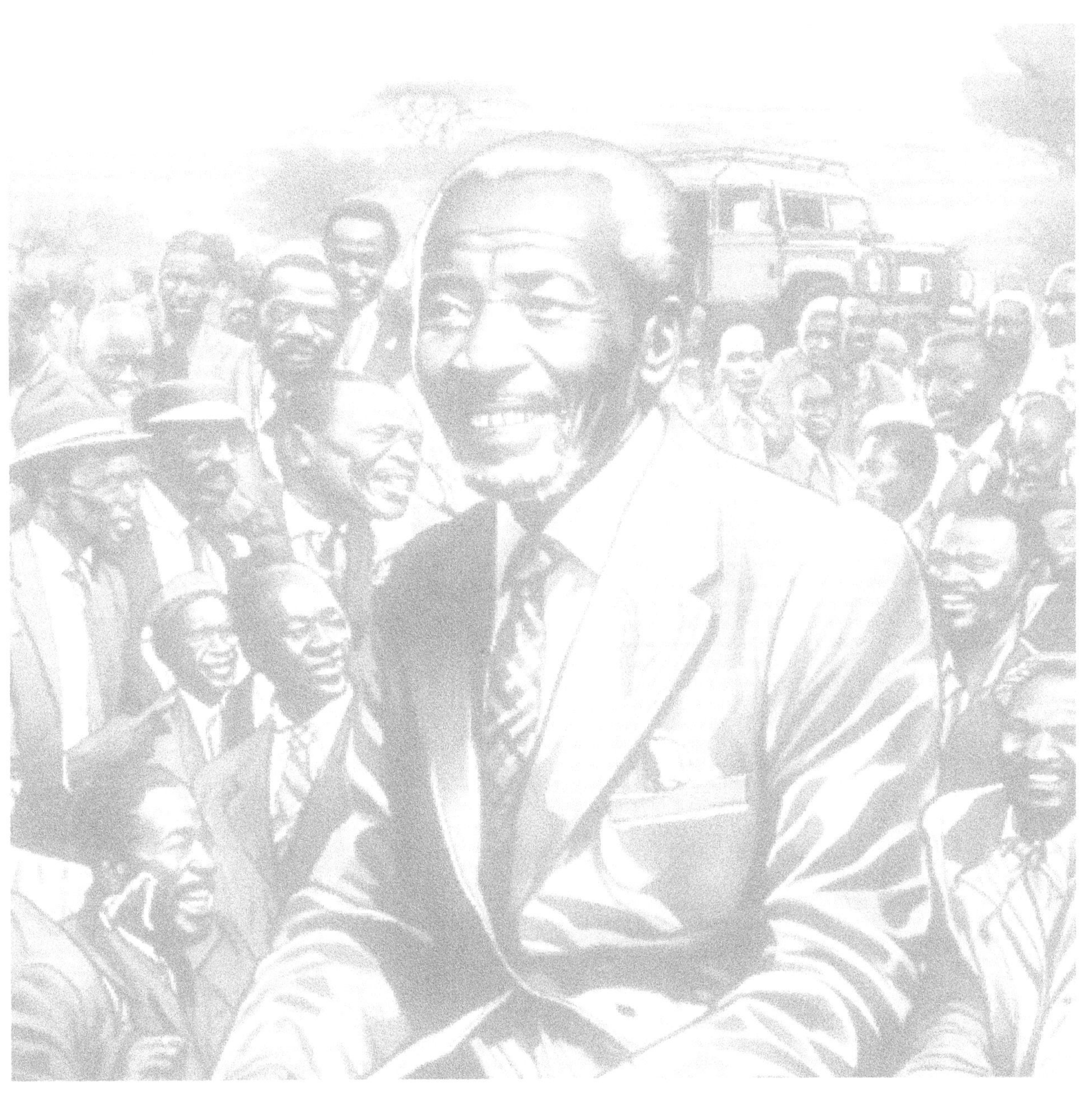

12 January 1962, Jomo Kenyatta was elected to the Legislative Council

EPISODE 8: LANCASTER HOUSE CONFERENCES

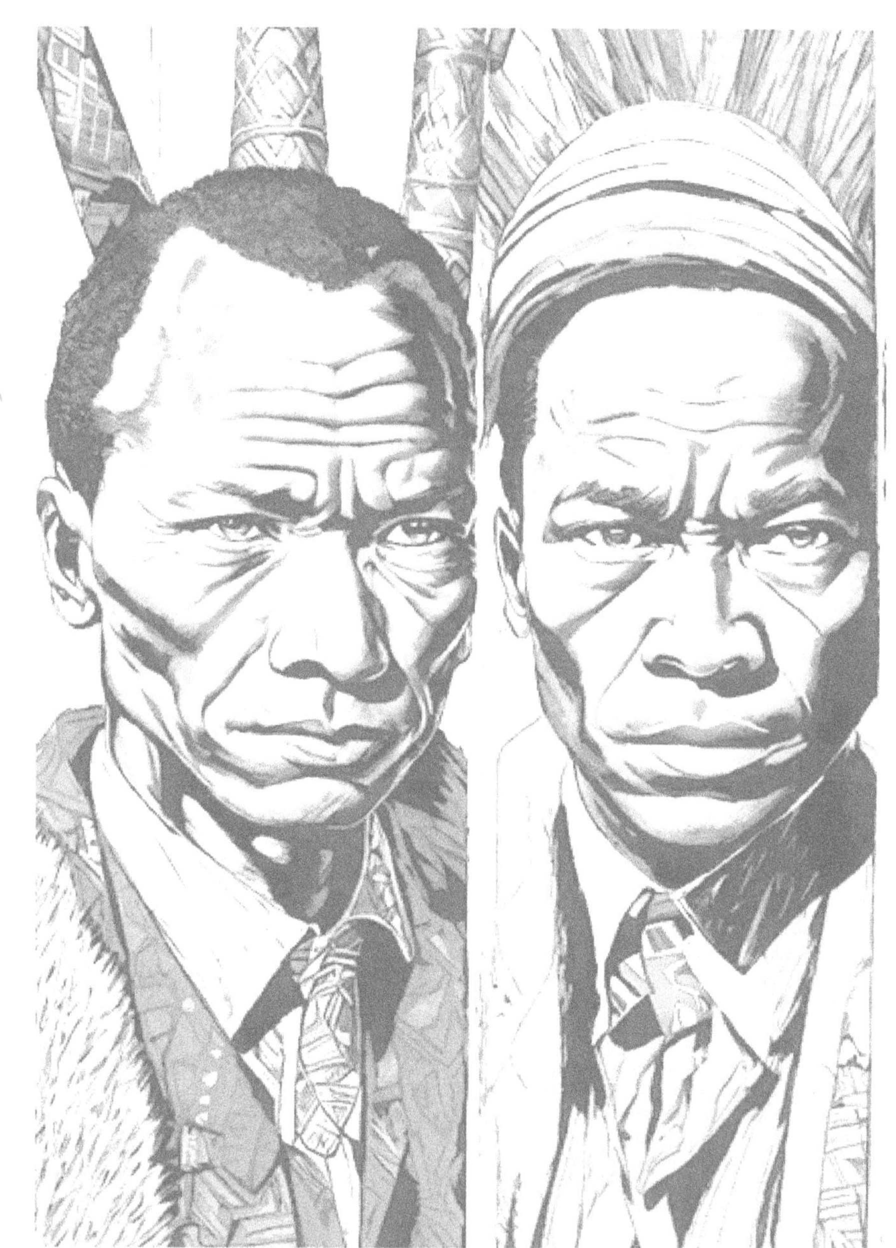

At the Independence Conference, the Maasai Elders sought a reversion of land rights once the British government had relinquished its control over Kenya

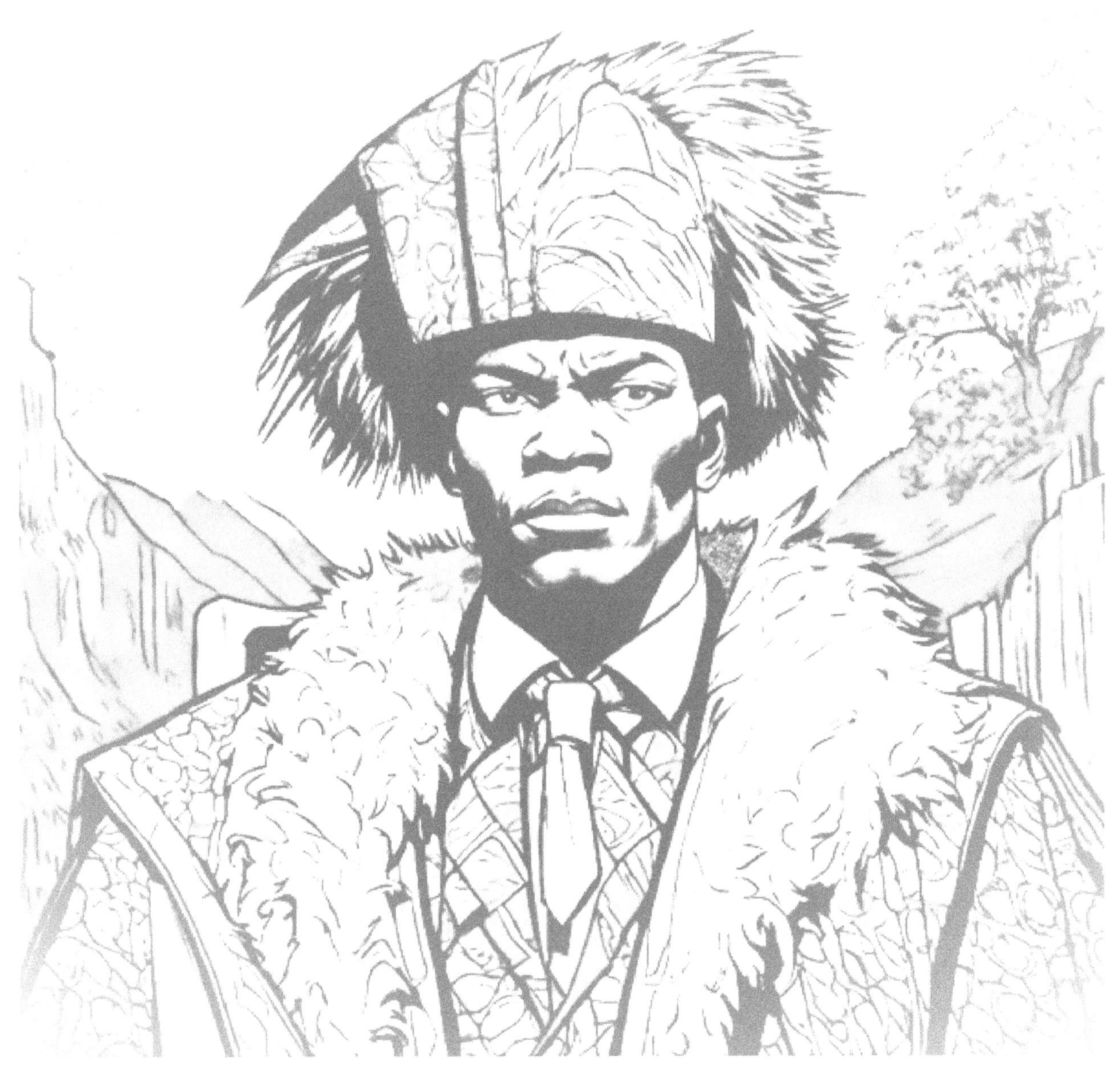

The Abaluyia community demanded re-unification, to include communities in Uganda, by removing or altering the 'artificial' inter-district, as well as international boundaries imposed under colonial rule.

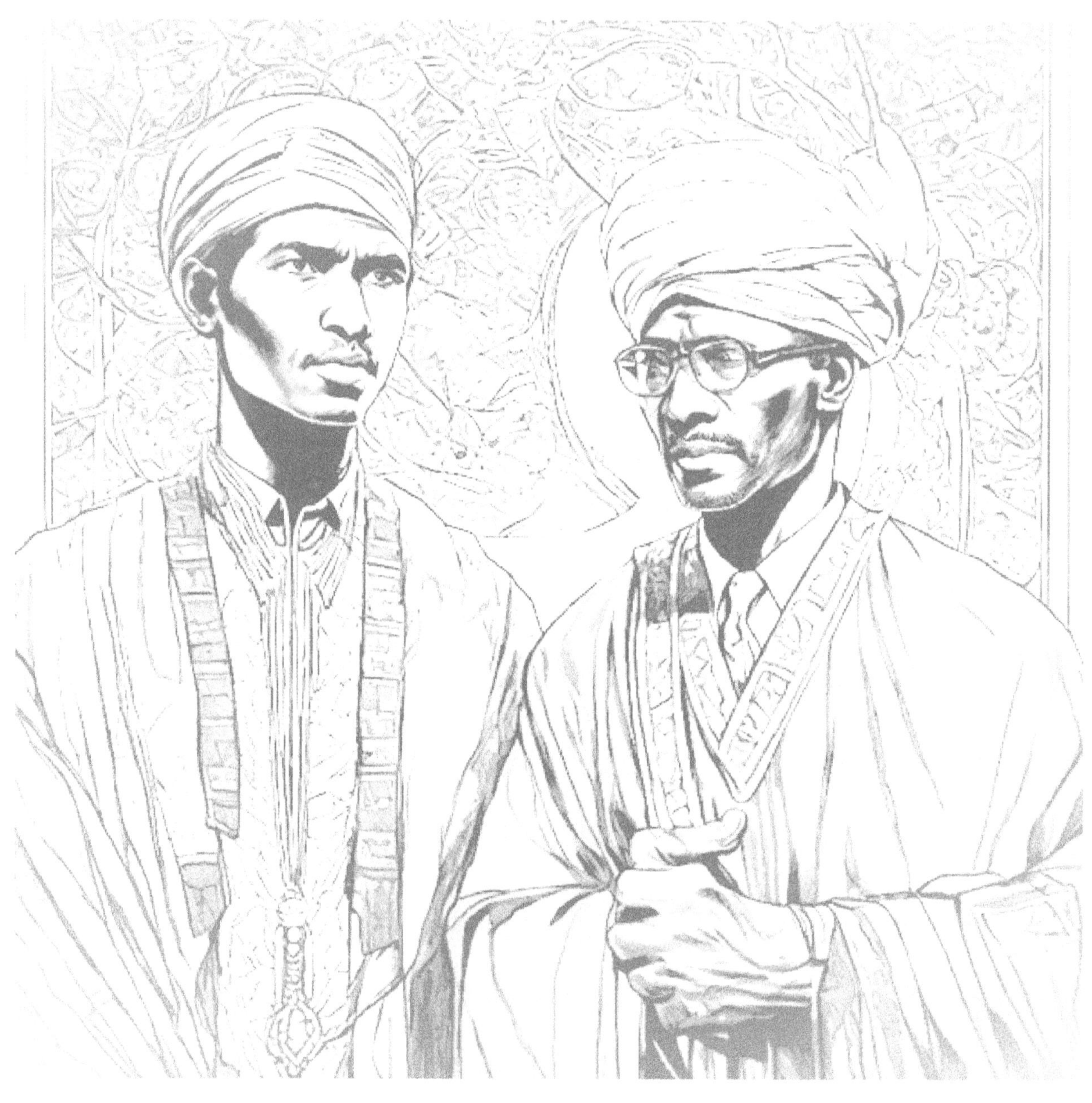

Somali Elders stated that the Northern Frontier District wished to secede and join the Somali Republic

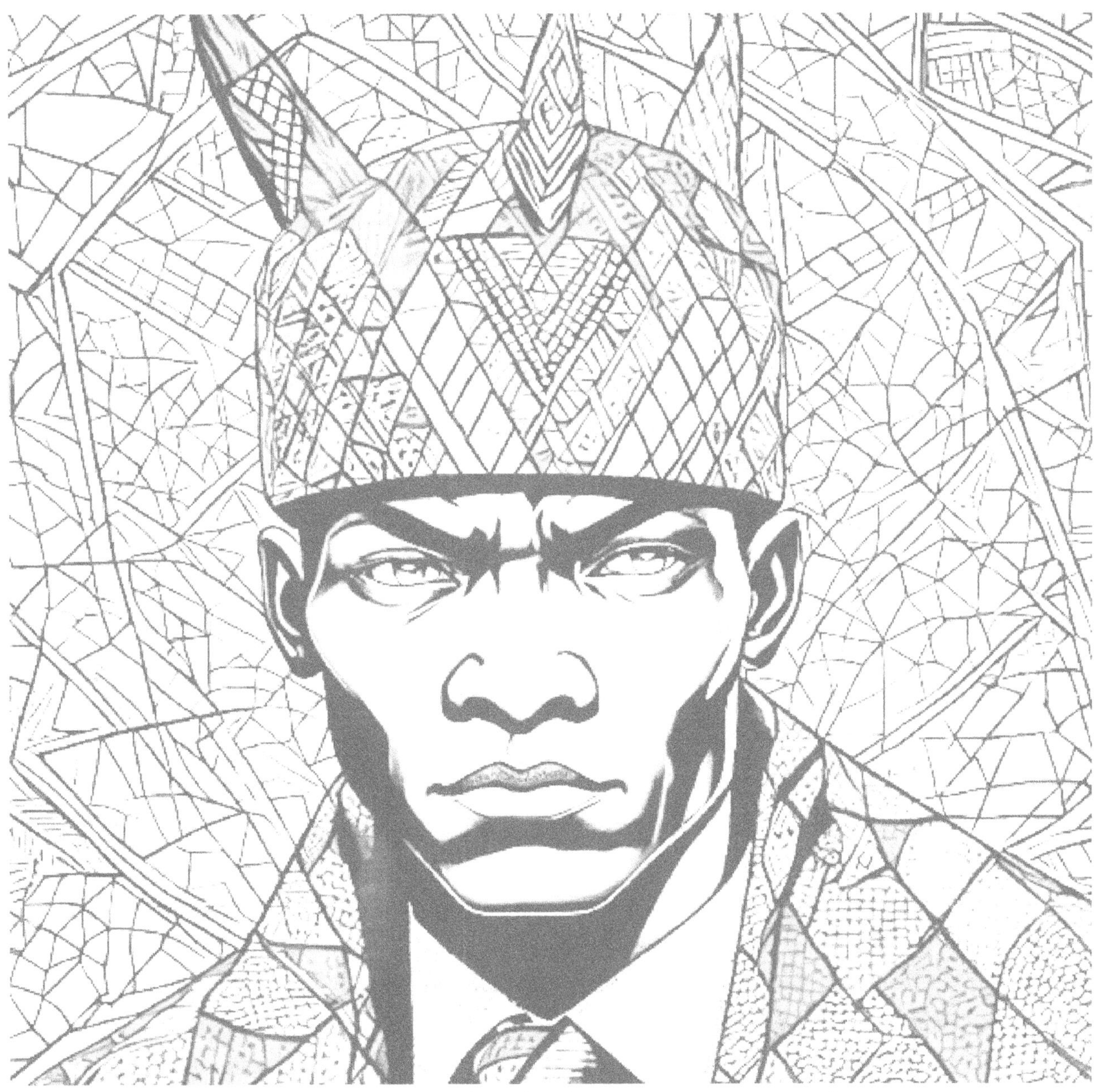

The party KADU wanted a federal system of government

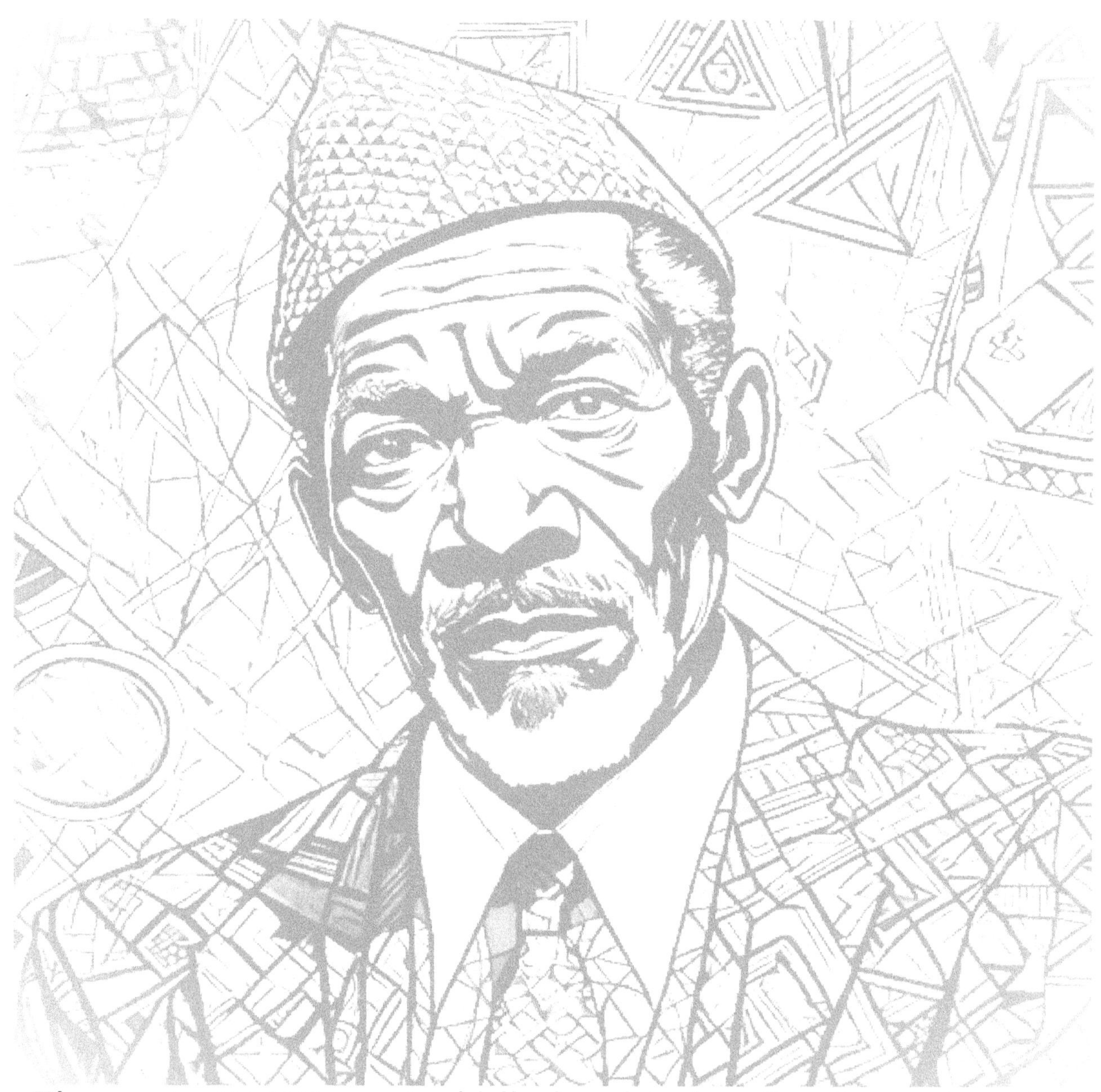

The party KANU wanted idle land to be distributed to the landless and poor Africans

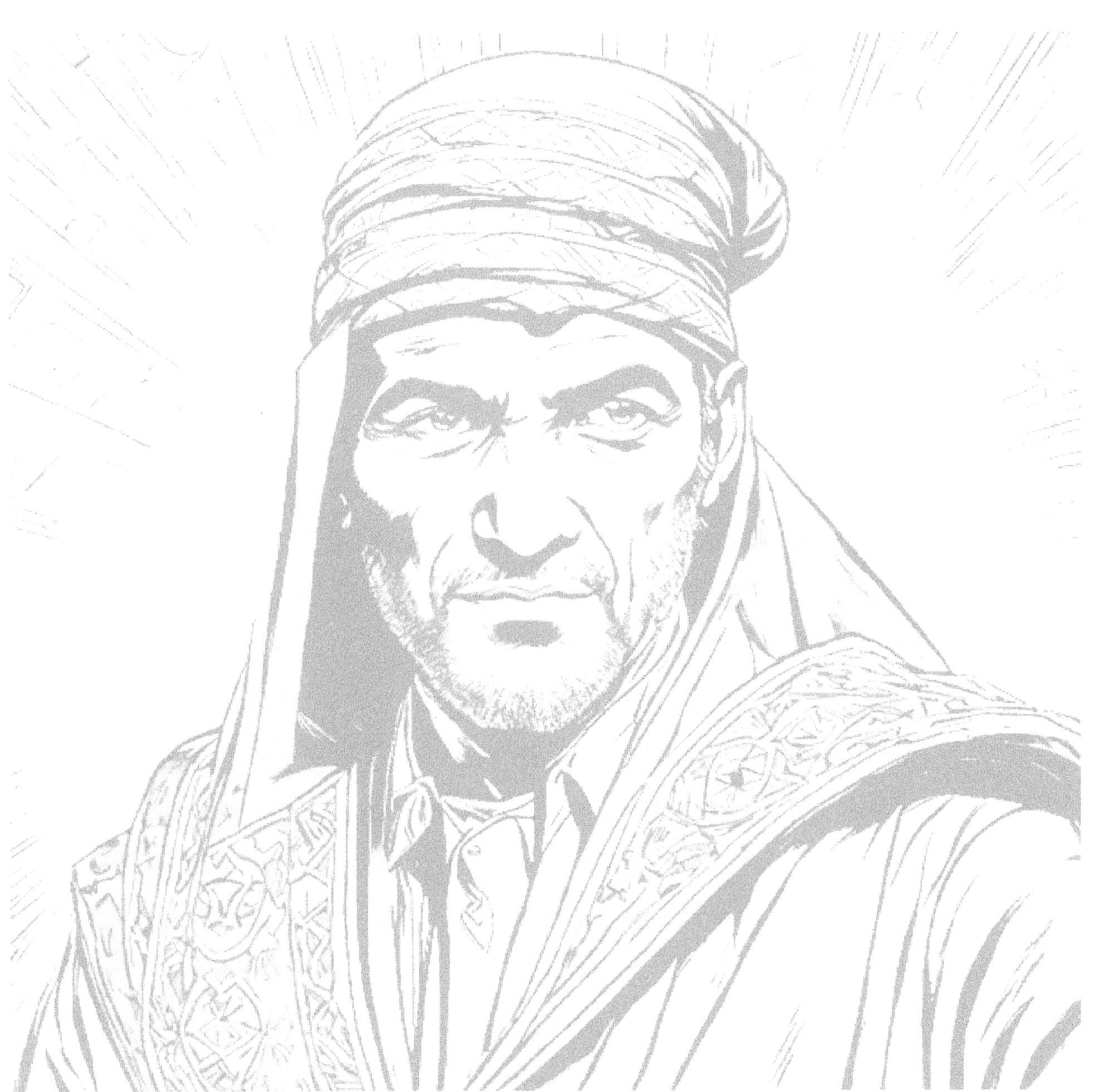

The Mwambao United Front reserved its memorandum until after the Conference on the Protectorate

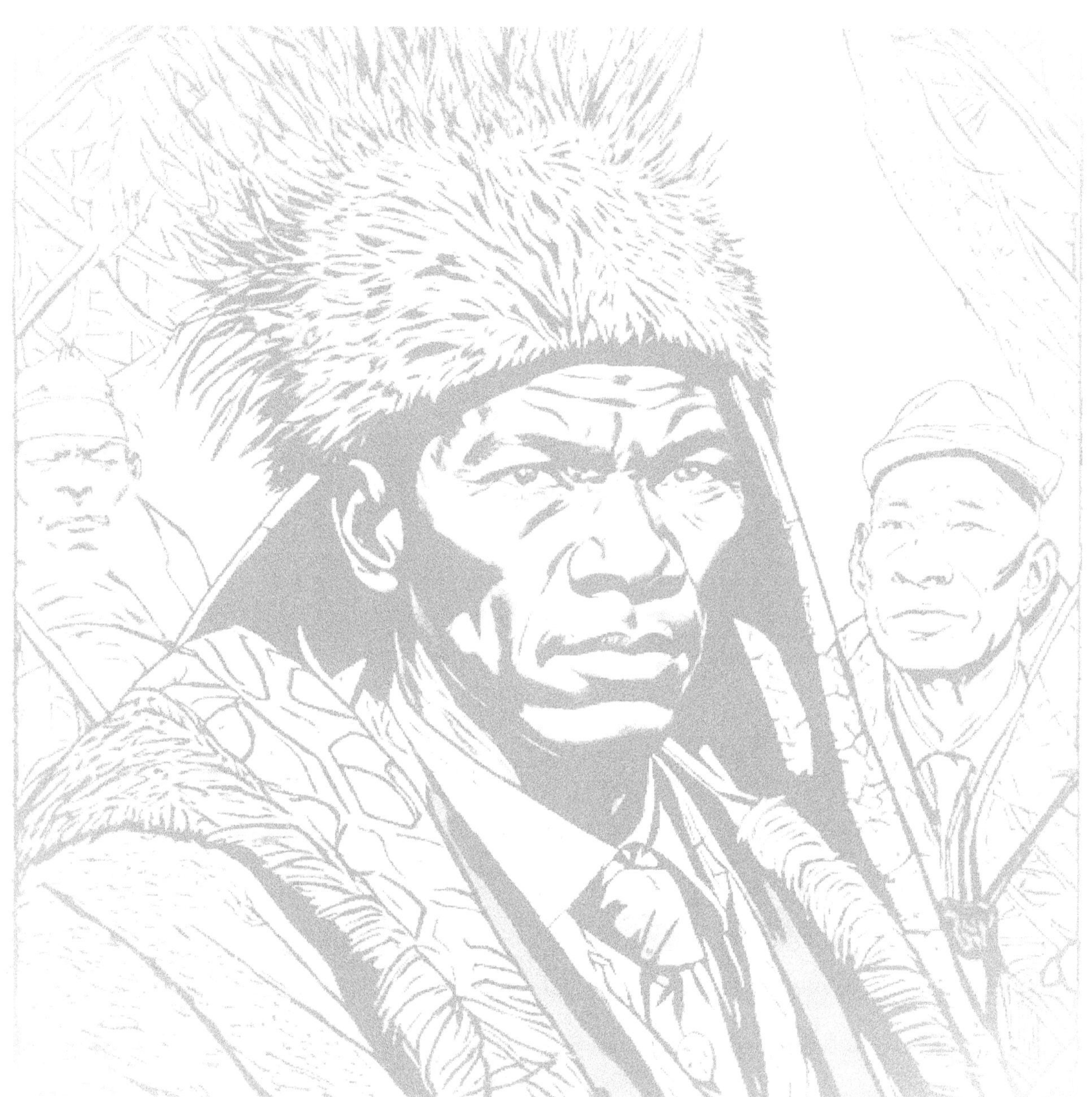

A Maasai Elder stated that KANU's memorandum had avoided dealing with pertinent issues

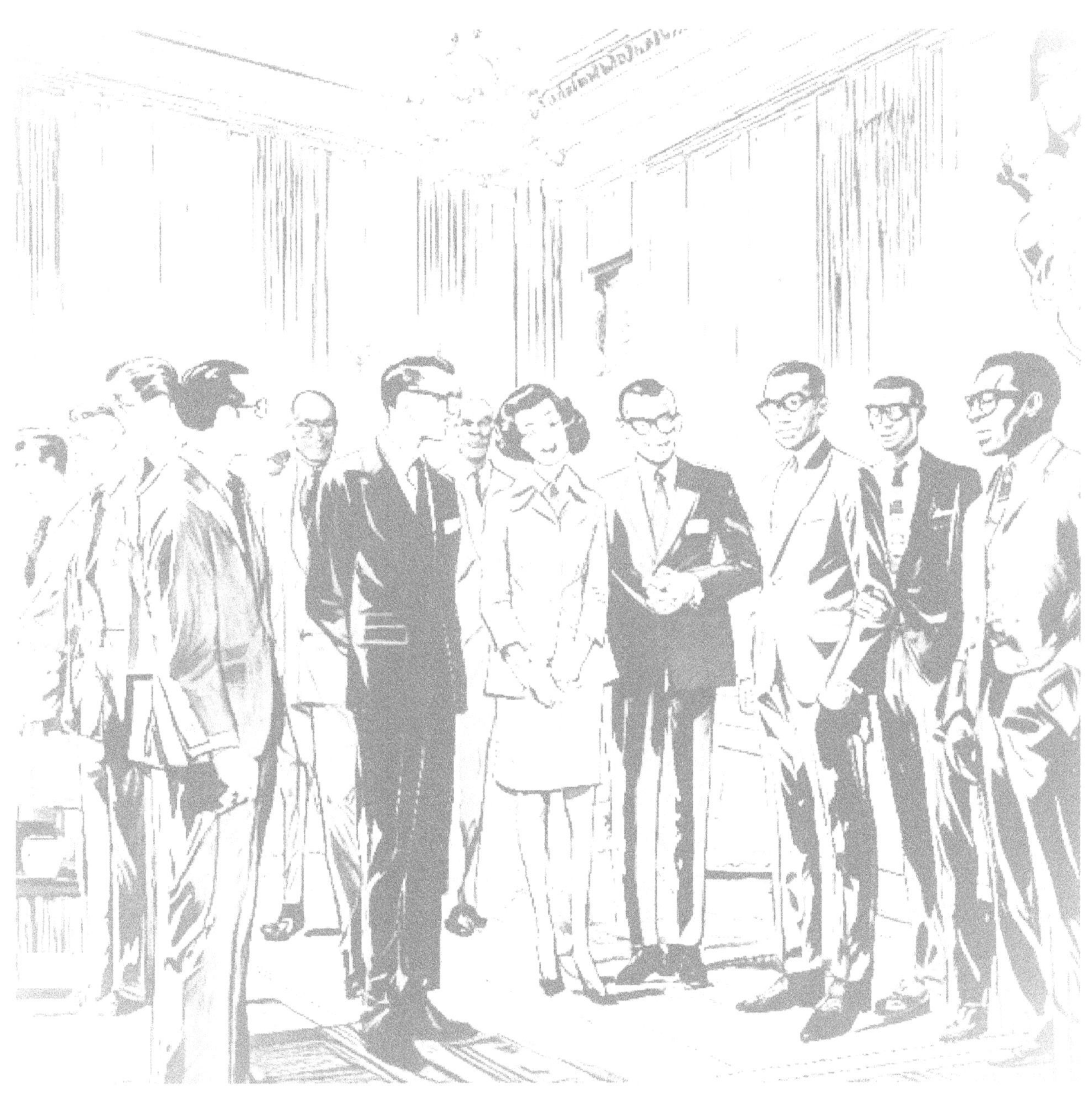

A Delegate to the Conference observed that there was a lot of 'cook work' that went on behind the scenes as the British prepared the transfer of power

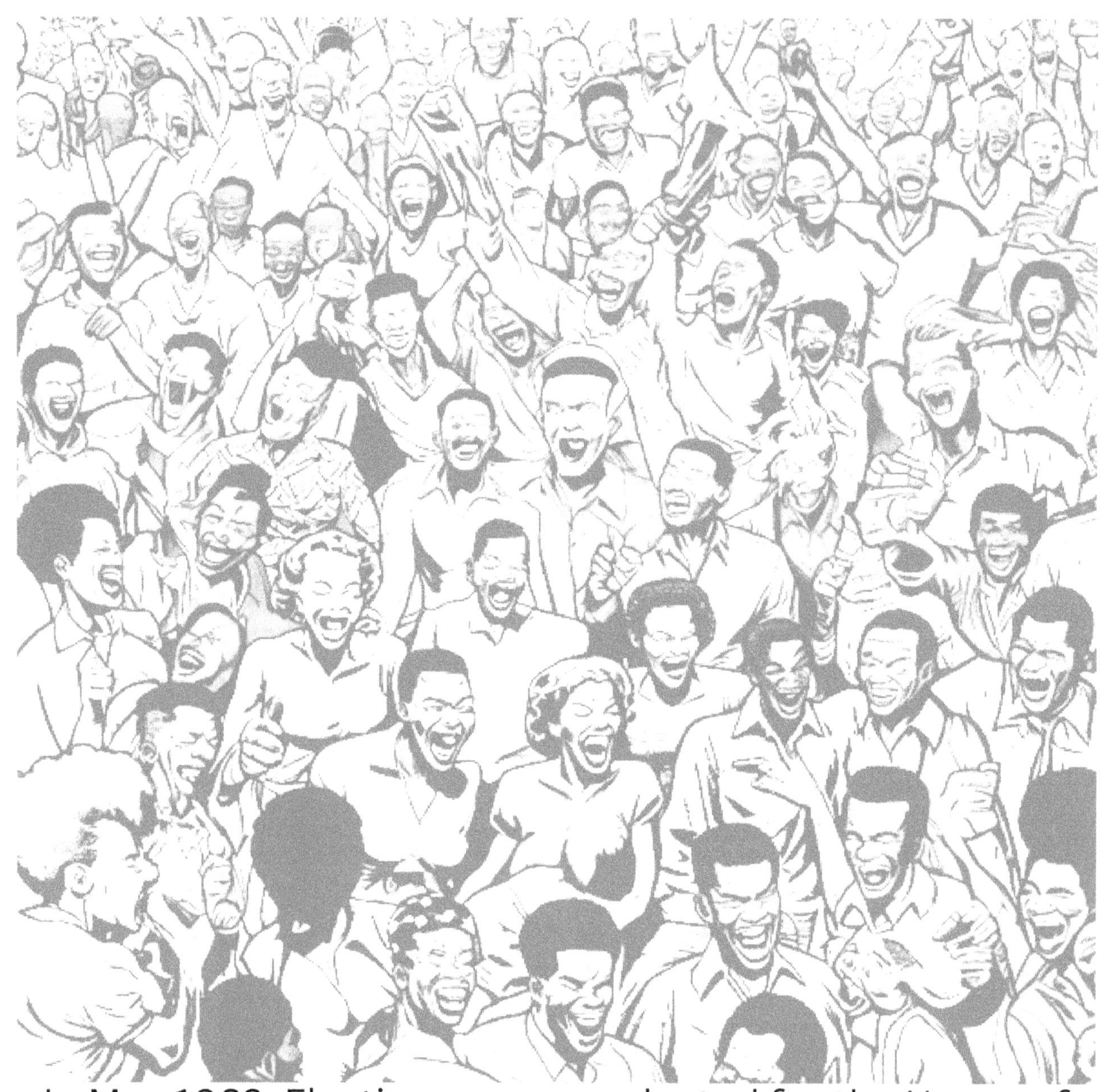

In May 1963, Elections were conducted for the House of Representatives and the Senate.

Kenya became a Republic on 12 December 1964

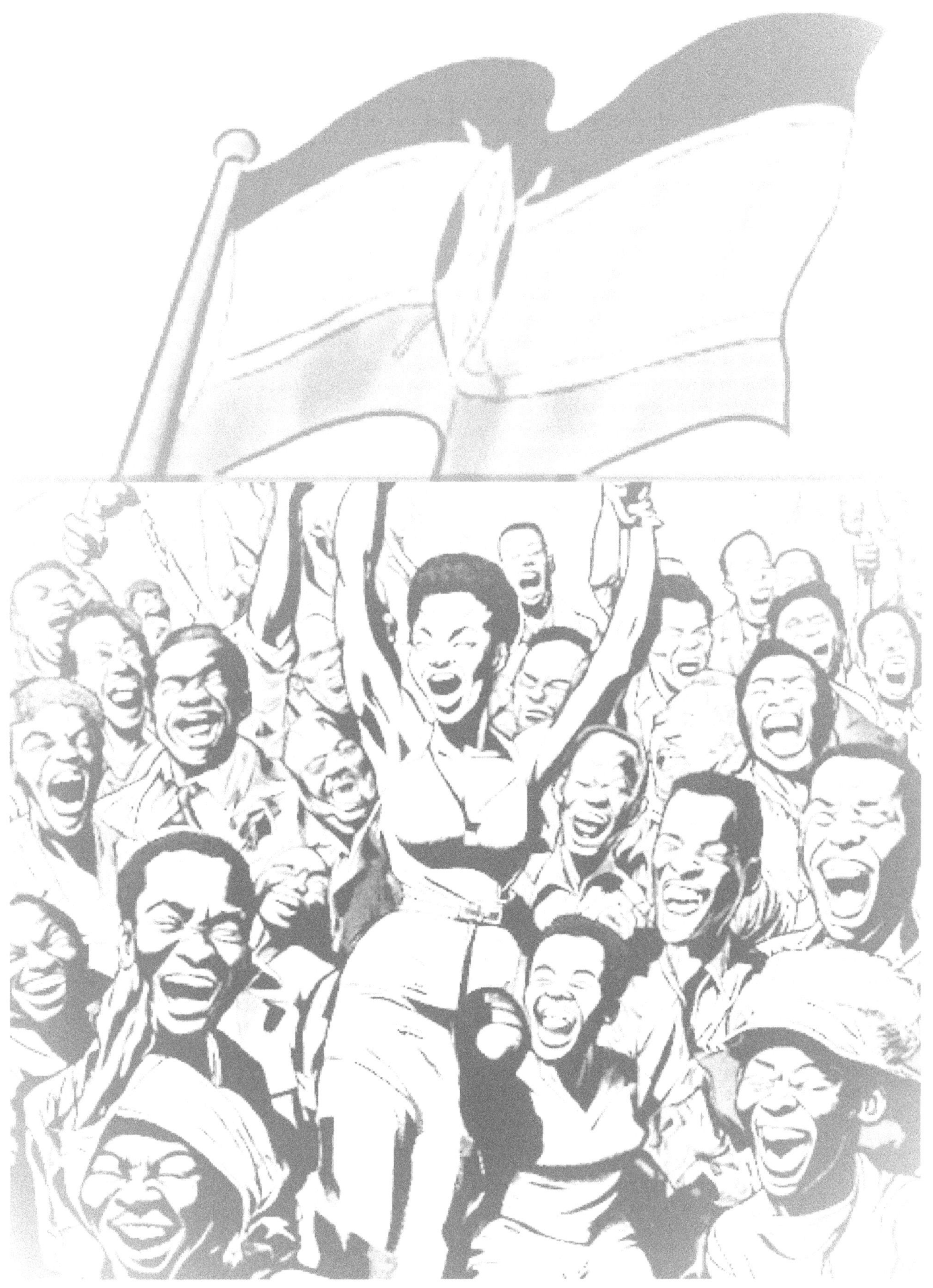

THE BEST
HISTORICAL BOOK
YOU ARE YET TO READ
VOLUME 1 & 2

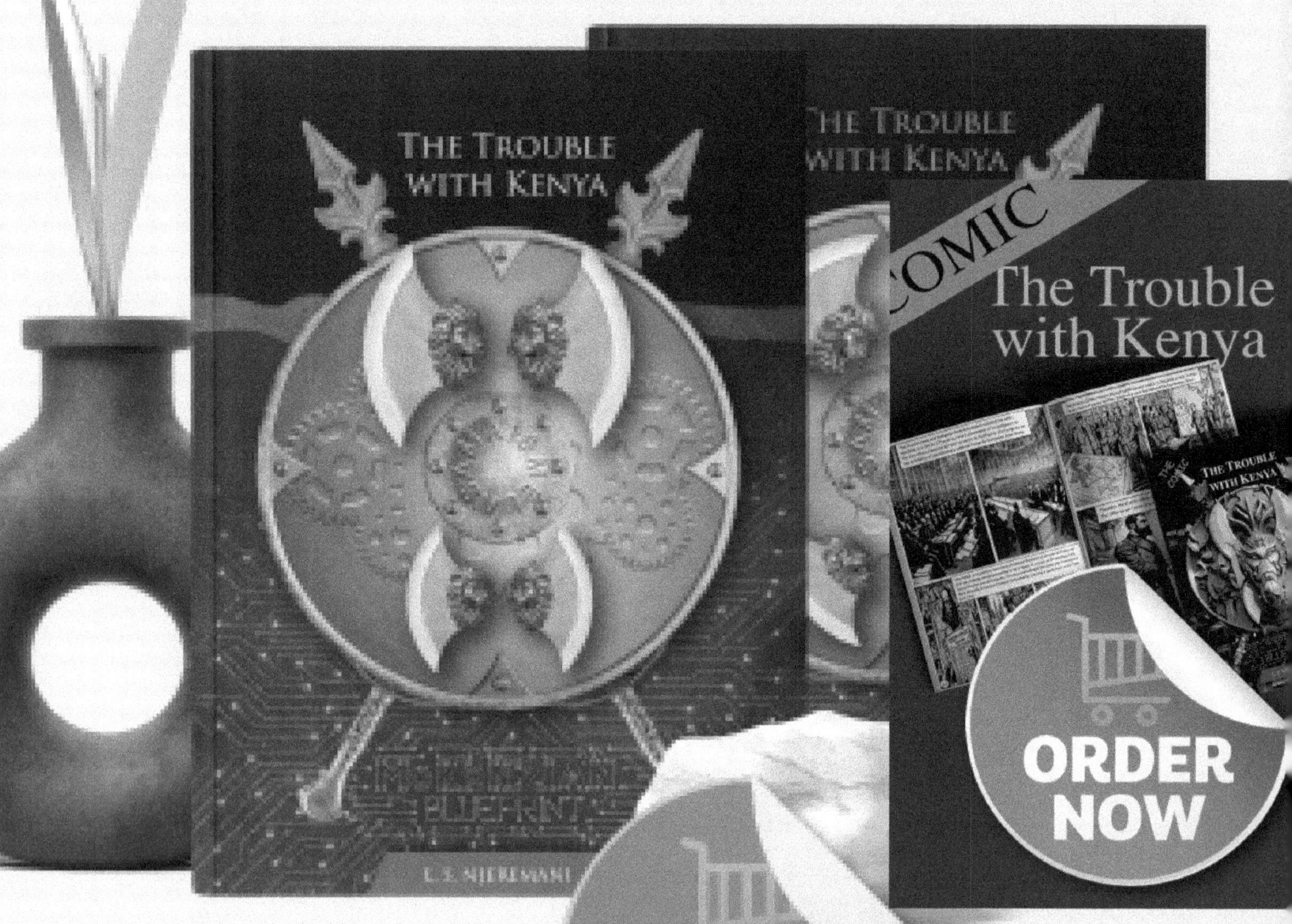

NOW AVAILABLE
AT YOUR FAVORITE BOOK POINT